Handbook of Intelligence and Guerrilla Warfare

Handbook
of
Intelligence
and
Guerrilla
Warfare

by *Alexander Orlov*

Ann Arbor   The University of Michigan Press

Preface

Before World War II, when I was one of the chiefs
of the Soviet intelligence, I lectured at the Central
Military School in Moscow on the tactics and strategy
of intelligence and counterintelligence. In 1936 I
wrote down the basic rules and principles of Soviet
intelligence in the form of a manual which was
approved as the only textbook for the newly created
NKVD schools for undercover intelligence officers and
for the Central Military School in Moscow.

Because intelligence has gained considerable
importance in world affairs and has become a regular
subject in the curricula of American and other
Western military colleges, the University of Michigan
Press has commissioned me with the reconstruction of
the intelligence manual. I did it in a way
that I thought would be suitable for the specialist
and the layman alike.

ALEXANDER ORLOV

New York

Contents

I. Two Doctrines

The importance of intelligence service in the fortunes of nations cannot be overstated. The United States learned this the hard way when it was caught by surprise at Pearl Harbor. This country had no secret agents in Japan to warn Washington of Japan's war plans and of the impending attack. The existence or absence of a well-working spy network on the territory of a potential enemy may spell the difference between victory and defeat. It is now known that the Russians, who long before World War II had taken pains to build up an effective network in Japan, received timely information from their underground resident in Tokyo, Richard Sorge, that Japan would not attack the Soviet Union but would definitely strike at the United States, "probably in December (1941), but not later than January, 1942."

The only people on whom the United States government depended for information at that crucial period were the American naval and military attachés in Tokyo. But the official attachés are rarely able to uncover the secret plans of a government to which they are accredited because the counterintelligence agencies of that government take special measures to impede the attempts of the attachés to collect vital information and often succeed in misleading them with misinformation. This is exactly what happened with the American naval attaché in Tokyo who informed Washington a day before the attack on Pearl Harbor that he did not expect a surprise attack because the Japanese fleet continued to be anchored at the main base of Yokosuka, as evidenced by large crowds of sailors in the streets of Tokyo. However, the naval attaché was grievously mistaken. At that very time the Japanese fleet was already well on its way to Pearl Harbor. The sailors crowding the streets of Tokyo were not sailors at all but soldiers dressed as navy men to deceive the Americans and conceal the departure of the fleet on its fateful mission.

Evidently due to the fact that the oceans surrounding this country had been regarded for centuries as impregnable defenses, this country was not overly preoccupied with building up its intelligence networks abroad and allowed its intelligence service to lag far behind those of other countries. General George C. Marshall frankly admitted at the Senate Committee on Military Affairs (Oct. 18, 1945) that until World War II the American intelligence abroad was "little more than what a military attaché could learn at a dinner, more or less, over the coffee cups." [1] When in 1941 President Roosevelt asked Colonel William J. Donovan to organize an intelligence service (the O.S.S.), he told Donovan: "You will have to begin with nothing. We have no intelligence service." [2] Dwight D. Eisenhower,[3] also deplored the "shocking deficiency" of American intelligence at the outset of

1 *Hearings,* "Department of Armed Forces," 79th Congress, 1st Session, Senate Committee on Military Affairs, Oct. 18, 1945.
2 William Donovan, "Intelligence: Key to Defense," *Life,* Sept. 30, 1946.
3 *Crusade in Europe* (New York, 1948), p. 32.

the war, and General Omar Bradley [4] stated that "the British easily outstripped their American colleagues" in military intelligence. The state of the so-called diplomatic intelligence was no less deplorable. Dean Acheson testified before a Congressional committee in 1945 that prior to World War II, the Department of State's "technique of gathering information differed only by reason of the typewriter and telegraph from the techniques which John Quincy Adams was using in St. Petersburg and Benjamin Franklin was using in Paris."

Till the advent of the atomic age, neglected intelligence and miscalculations resulting from it could lead a country to serious debacles and even to partial defeat, but the character and tempo of war were such that the country could still mobilize in a hurry and, while holding off the enemy, build up its weapons production and get ready for the final showdown. When Hitler started World War II, Germany greatly outnumbered the Allies in tanks, planes, and armored divisions. Hitler hoped by blitzkrieg strategy to achieve a quick victory before the Allies had time to mobilize and arm themselves. However, the Allies made good use of the precious element of time that was running out and converted their industrial might to arms production. The United States proclaimed itself the "arsenal of democracy" and, having put its enormous productive capacity at the disposal of the Allies, outproduced the Axis in war planes, tanks, ships, and everything else.

The introduction of nuclear weapons and ballistic missiles capable of wiping out whole cities and industrial centers in a single attack has radically changed

4 *A Soldier's Story* (New York, 1951), p. 33.

the nature of war. The *time element,* which previously allowed a country that lagged behind to catch up with the enemy, no longer exists. There is no longer any margin for error. A world power which is determined to survive cannot allow itself to fall behind its potential enemy in striking or retaliatory power. A major scientific breakthrough in the field of weaponry achieved by one side and unnoticed by the other may spell defeat for the country whose intelligence service slept on the job.

The country unable to pinpoint the exact location of the missile sites of the enemy loses the power to retaliate, a circumstance which may embolden the enemy to attack without fear of reprisals. Under these perilous conditions, when countries possess the means to break each other's backbones with a single nuclear stroke, no responsible government can allow itself to conduct its foreign affairs blindly. As the Hoover Commission rightly concluded in its findings, "the fate of the Nation may well rest on accurate and complete intelligence data which may serve as a trustworthy guide for top-level decisions on policy and action in a troubled world . . ." [5] Since 1955, when this was written, new conquests have been made in space, new weapons have been added to the arsenals of the big powers, and the international situation has gravely deteriorated.

To remain in the dark today about the intentions and the military capabilities of a potential enemy is a sure way to national disaster. That is why the role of intelligence in our critical times has become more cru-

5   *Intelligence Activities,* p. 25, Commission on Organization of the Executive Branch of the Government, Report to Congress, June 1955.

cial than ever before in history. This is equally true in relation to the two mightiest powers, the Soviet Union and the United States, which confront each other in the titanic contest that is shaping up in the world. Since an intelligence gap may be as fatal to a country as a missile gap, it would be very useful to try to gauge and compare the performance of the intelligence agencies of the countries of the Soviet bloc and of the West. But this lies outside the scope of this volume. Here I shall limit myself to the examination of the difference between the intelligence doctrines adopted by the intelligence services of the Russians and of their Western rivals.

Like the Western intelligence services, the Russians collect information about foreign states from two principal sources: from secret informants and undercover agents and from legitimate sources—such as military and scientific journals, various research material, records of parliamentary debates, etc. The Russians regard as true intelligence (*razvedka*) only the first type of information—procured by undercover agents and secret informants in defiance of the laws of the foreign country in which they operate. The second type of information, obtained from legitimate sources and publications, is considered by the Russians simply as *research data*. According to the views of Russian officers, it takes a *man* to do the creative and highly dangerous work of underground intelligence on foreign soil; as to the digging up of research data in the safety of the home office or library, this can be left to women or young lieutenants who have just begun intelligence careers. The Western intelligence services on the other hand treat both types of information as intelligence, often with a much higher regard for research than for undercover work.

It is in the attitude of the Soviet and Western intelligence agencies toward these two types of information that the difference between their intelligence doctrines begins to emerge. This difference is not only theoretical, but is tied pragmatically to every phase of intelligence activity, beginning with matters of planning, strategy, and evaluation of the procured information, from the point of view of reliability and its worth, to policymaking by leaders of the state.

Both the Soviet and the Western intelligence services strive to obtain information about the secret intentions, capabilities, and strategic plans of other states. But the Soviets and the West approach this task differently. The Russians take the view that important secrets of foreign states can and should be procured directly from the classified files in the government departments of those states and from foreign civil servants who agree to turn over state secrets to the Soviet Union. When the Russians suspect that another country is trying to form a coalition against the Soviet Union, they do not seek information about it in newspaper editorials, panel discussions, or in historical precedents that show how the countries concerned had acted in similar situations in the past, although all these sources may be enlightening to a certain extent. The Russian intelligence service goes out to steal the secret diplomatic correspondence between the conspiring states or to recruit a secret informant on the staff of the negotiators if they do not have one there already. When the Russians want to know the number of bombers in the air force of a potential adversary, they arrive at a figure—not by library research on the productive capacity of certain plants or by collecting educated guesses or rumors on the subject but by interviewing their secret informers in the foreign air force or war ministry and by stealing the coveted information from governmental files.

On the other hand, the Americans, and to a certain extent the British, prefer to rely more heavily in their intelligence work on the collection of information about foreign states from legitimately accessible sources, such as library research, foreign newspapers, military and scientific journals, foreign parliamentary debates, encyclopedias, and statistics. According to a reliable source, the American intelligence agencies monitor as many as five million words daily from foreign radio broadcasts alone (which equals fifty books of average length) and condense them into a few short pages which are forwarded to interested departments. From that enormous backlog of material obtained through legitimate research, the intelligence officers and trained analysts derive, process, and distill much information about foreign countries, their economies and finances, industries, agriculture and trade, populations and social trends, education, political systems, structure of governments, and biographical data on political and military leaders. Drawing on that colossal collection of data, the intelligence officers write intelligence reports and estimates of situations under study and compose the so-called *national estimates* of foreign countries for the benefit of the government policymakers.

Admiral Ellis Zacharias, who was deputy chief of Naval Intelligence in World War II, wrote that in the Navy 95 per cent of peacetime intelligence was derived from legitimately accessible sources, another four per cent came from semiopen sources, and only one per cent was procured through secret agents.[6] This means that the Navy had no network of spies and secret agents and apparently preferred to base its intelligence work on legitimate sources. Another authority on American intelligence, General William J. Donovan, who headed the Office of Strategic Services (O.S.S.) during the war, expressed the same predilection of American intelligence toward "open sources" by saying that intelligence is not the "mysterious, even sinister" thing people think it is, but is more a matter of "pulling together myriad facts, making a pattern of them, and drawing inferences from that pattern." [7]

This predilection of American intelligence toward "open sources"—as opposed to networks of spies and undercover agents—lies at the core of the *American doctrine of intelligence.*

How can the intelligence officers pick important developments from the vast encyclopedic data that flow into the intelligence agency? One of the chiefs of American intelligence, a distinguished professor and noted scholar, had this to say on the subject:

"How can surveillance (of the world scene) assure itself of spotting really the unusual?" wrote he. "How can it be sure of putting the finger on the three things per week out of the thousands it observes and the millions that happen that are really of potential import? The answer is: procure the services of wise men—and

6   Captain Ellis M. Zacharias, U.S.N., *Secret Missions, the Story of an Intelligence Officer* (New York: G. P. Putnam's Sons, 1946), pp. 117–18.
7   Recently published works estimate that American intelligence agencies obtain about 80–90 per cent of its information from publicly accessible sources and only 10–20 per cent from secret sources.

wise in the subject—and *pray that their mysterious inner selves are of the kind which produce hypotheses of national importance."*

From the point of view of the Russian intelligence doctrine, such an approach is but one step removed from mysticism and metaphysics. And what if the "mysterious inner selves" of the researchers and analysts fail to produce the right hypotheses? How safe is it, in general, to rely on hypotheses in matters of such profound complexity as world politics, involving a multiplicity of factors, where nothing is stable, and when enemies of yesterday become friends of today and together fight their former allies? A hypothesis may be wisdom itself, except for one thing: it may turn out to be utterly wrong. Not only intelligence officers but statesmen of the highest caliber have time and again been proved wrong when they acted on undeniably wise hypotheses. Thus, for instance, in 1940–41 Stalin based his strategy on the assumption that Hitler would not attack the Soviet Union. Stalin's calculations seemed eminently right, because he knew that it was not in the interests of Germany to get into a two-front war and to take on mighty Russia while at war with England, America, and France. Stalin thought that Hitler understood this too. But as it has turned out, Stalin's logical hypothesis went up in smoke and fires ignited by the bombs of the German Luftwaffe. In the spring of 1941, when the German General Staff began to deploy armored divisions near the Russian borders and Europe was thick with rumors that Germany was getting ready to attack Russia, the British intelligence service was ordered to give its estimate of the situation. The Joint Intelligence Committee of Britain also thought that Hitler would not be so foolish as to add the powerful Soviet Union to his formidable enemies in the West and concluded that Germany would not invade Russia. Many more examples could be introduced to show how dangerous it is, especially in matters of war and peace, to rely on hypotheses or assumptions which may be truly wise, but wrong in the end.

Stalin, who was his own intelligence boss and who liked to take a personal part in the cloak and dagger business, warned his intelligence chiefs time and again to keep away from hypotheses and "equations with many unknowns" and, instead, to strive to acquire valuable informants and to get at the facts and figures hidden in the secret vaults of foreign governments. He used to say: "An intelligence hypothesis may become your hobby-horse on which you will ride straight into a self-made trap." He called it "dangerous guesswork." For that very reason Stalin in 1932 ordered intelligence to discontinue sending him quarterly surveys of foreign countries which, although based on secret data, were interspersed with unsubstantiated assumptions and subjective views. These surveys corresponded roughly to the *national estimates* which the American intelligence agencies produce for the National Security Council. Thereafter, the NKVD sent Stalin only summaries of important documents stolen from other governments and reports from exceptionally valuable secret informants of the caliber of foreign ambassadors and general staff officers. During his periodic conferences with the chiefs of the intelligence services, Stalin would often interject: "Don't tell me what you think, give me the facts and the source!" But sometimes he would violate his own rule and ask one or another intelligence chief for an opinion. Such was the case during a joint conference which Stalin and Voroshilov had in the summer of 1936 with the chiefs of the NKVD Intelligence and the Intelligence Department of the Red Army. Stalin asked Artouzov, deputy chief of the military intelligence, the following question: "With whom will Poland side if war breaks out between two coalitions, Germany, Italy and Japan, on the one side, and Russia, France and England, on the other?" Without hesitation Artouzov answered: "Poland will always be with France and England!"—"You are a jackass," retorted Stalin. "If Poland does not side with Germany against us, she will be crushed by the German mechanized divisions on their way to the Soviet Union, and Poland will not live to see another day, whereas if Poland allies herself with Germany, she can hope to expand, if things go well, and, if things go badly, she might still get a chance to negotiate for a settlement." Artouzov did not live to see his prediction come true. He was shot in the great purge, in 1937.

The NKVD Intelligence had never gone into research or studies of publicly available material and based its work 100 per cent on secret sources and undercover agents.[8] The Main Intelligence Department of the Army did study materials from legitimately accessible sources, but only those that dealt with military problems, such as foreign military and scientific journals, army and navy manuals, military textbooks, topographic explorations, and everything that appeared in print anywhere about the armed forces of the world. However, at least 80 per cent of the main

8   In the Soviet Union research from publicly accessible sources is conducted by the Academy of Sciences, universities, scientific journals, and the ministries of Foreign Affairs, industry, trade, finance, and statistics.

efforts of the army intelligence were concentrated on building and operating networks of secret informants and on procuring secret information about the state and strategic plans of the armed forces of various countries.

Had the Soviet intelligence agencies expended their main efforts and resources on building up extensive encyclopedias of worldwide information from overt sources and on processing and analyzing that enormous amount of incoming physical material, they would have never been able to acquire the secrets of the manufacture of the atomic and hydrogen bombs or the blueprints of the American nuclear-powered submarines, nor infiltrate the key departments of the American, British, and other European governments. Important state secrets and especially clues to the intentions and plans of potential enemies *cannot be found in libraries or encyclopedias,* but only where they are being kept under lock and key. The task of intelligence services is to acquire the keys and lay the secrets before their governments and thus provide them with *foreknowledge* and orientation needed to make decisions.

When General Douglas MacArthur, who had been blamed for not having foreseen certain developments in the Korean War, was asked at the Senate investigating committee, in 1951, to explain why the North Korean invasion caught the Americans by surprise, he gave a classical reply from which many an intelligence chief could take his cue. He said: "I don't see how it would have been humanly possible for any men or group of men to predict such an attack as that . . . *There is nothing, no means or methods, except* the accidental *spy methods—if you can get somebody to betray the enemy's highest circles, that can get such information as that.* It is guarded with a secrecy that you cannot overestimate." [9]

Thus, under the fire of the investigation, General MacArthur, who was not an expert in intelligence, mastered his excellent logic and advanced an idea which touches the very nerve of the intelligence problem. *"There is nothing, no means or methods, except . . . spy methods . . . that can get such information as that."* This brings us back to the very essence of the Soviet doctrine of intelligence.

9 *Hearings,* "Military Situation in the Far East," Senate Committees on Armed Services and Foreign Relations, 82nd Congress, 1st Session, May 5, 1951, Part 1, p. 240.

II. Targets of Soviet Intelligence

Two separate organizations of the Soviet government are engaged in intelligence operations abroad. They are *The Foreign Directorate of the Committee of State Security* (KGB) and *The Main Intelligence Department* (GRU) of the Soviet Ministry of Defense. But while the Intelligence Department of the armed forces conducts only military intelligence, the Foreign Directorate of the Committee of State Security (KGB) is actively engaged in at least eight lines of intelligence and related fields, including military intelligence as well.

The first line, which is considered the most important, is the so-called *diplomatic intelligence,* the purpose of which is to keep the Soviet government informed of the secret deals between the governments of capitalistic countries and of the true intentions and contemplated moves of each of those governments toward the Soviet Union. It is the duty of the Soviet intelligence to procure this information not on the basis of hearsay stories, rationalizations, or speculations, but from primary sources within the secret councils of foreign governments and thus provide the Kremlin with a firm basis of *foreknowledge,* on which to plan and formulate its own policies.

The principal sources of diplomatic intelligence are foreign diplomats, including ambassadors; staff members of foreign ministries, including code clerks and secretaries; private secretaries to members of the cabinet; and members of parliaments and ambitious politicians who in their quest for political power seek financial aid and left-wing support. The Soviet intelligence studies closely the life history of foreign high officials beginning with their school years, their character traits, weaknesses and vices, intimate lives, and friendships. All this is analyzed with the purpose of finding the Achilles heel of the official and securing the right approach to him through the proper person, who may be a former classmate, an intimate friend, or relative.

In many cases these well-prepared approaches paid off. Some politicians were lured into the Soviet network by promises that the Soviet Union would use its secret levers of influence in their countries to further their political fortunes. These promises were often accompanied by "subsidies," ostensibly for the purpose of promoting good will toward Russia, but in reality intended as a bribe. A number of high officials succumbed to outright offers of money. Others, especially those who in their youth had belonged to Fabian and other idealistic circles, were influenced by humanitarian reasons and persuaded that they must help the Soviet Union to stop the march of Fascism and avert a world war. Considerable success was achieved by the Soviet intelligence among foreign diplomats tinted with homosexual perversions. It is no secret that the biggest concentration of homosexuals can be found in the diplomatic services of Western countries. The Soviet intelligence has made ample use of these unstable individuals. Those of them who agreed to work for the Russian network were instructed to approach other homosexual members of the diplomatic corps, a strategy which was remarkably successful. Even in those cases where some of the approached declined the offer to collaborate, they did not denounce the recruiter to the authorities. The Soviet intelligence officers were amazed at the sense of mutual consideration and true loyalty among homosexuals.

It is usually thought that it is much easier to lure into the Soviet network a code clerk or secretary than a diplomat or statesman. This viewpoint sounds logical enough, since a man in an important government position is expected to know better than take the road of treachery; and, besides, he has much more to lose, if caught. However, the experience of the Soviet intelligence has, in too many instances, not borne out this point of view. Honesty and loyalty may be often more deeply ingrained in the make-up of simple and humble people than in men of high position. A man who was taking bribes when he was a patrolman does not turn honest when he becomes the chief of police. The only thing that changes is the size of the bribe. Weakness of character and inability to withstand temptation remain with the man no matter how high he climbs. Lightmindedness, wishful thinking, and bad judgment are also traits that accompany the man to the highest rungs of his career.

The consensus of Soviet intelligence chiefs has been that departmental and private secretaries in a foreign ministry are often more valuable as sources of information than an ambassador, because a well-placed secretary can supply documentary data on a wider scale, covering the policies of the foreign government toward a number of countries. However, an ambassador is considered a much bigger prize because he can be used not only as a source of information, but also as a competent consultant for the Russian Foreign Office, as well as an agent who can influence to a certain extent the foreign policy of his government in the direction desired by the Kremlin.

The second line of the Soviet intelligence activities is *Military Intelligence*. Its task is to procure data on the military strength of Western and Eastern countries; the qualitative and quantitative state of their armies, navies, and air forces; the degree of mechanization, mobility, fire power, technological advancement, and modernization; the productive capacity of the armament industries and the mobilization plans of the big powers.

Soviet intelligence watches with a jealous eye every new invention in the field of arms that appears on the horizon and strives to steal it while it is still in the blueprint stage, or on the drawing board, to enable the Soviet inventors and engineers to come up with the invention first. With the advent of the nuclear and rocketry age, which has completely revolutionized the material base, the strategy, and the very concept of warfare, the Soviet intelligence strains all its efforts to obtain immediate information on the progress being made by the leading Western countries in these decisive fields and to gauge the striking and retaliatory power of the Western world.

Unlike the Main Intelligence Department of the Soviet Army, the Foreign Directorate of the KGB does not look for information in publicly available sources. Neither is it interested in monitoring foreign radio transmissions and distilling from them crumbs of random information. The Foreign Directorate of the KGB procures the military secrets of foreign governments from the classified files of the general staffs of those countries, from the secret reports of foreign defense ministries, and from military research laboratories and proving grounds. The Foreign Directorate obtains this information the hard way, but when it gets it, no matter how incomplete, the Directorate knows that the data received contain true facts on which the Soviet policy-makers can confidently base conclusions and decisions.

It must be said here that although the Main Intelligence Department of the Soviet Army shares the same practice with Western intelligence services in that it conducts paper research and digests a lot of published material, it lays the principal stress on procuring intelligence from covert sources by clandestine means in the same way as it is done by the Foreign Directorate of the KGB.

In wartime, military intelligence becomes the principal function of every branch of the Intelligence Directorate of the KGB. The main task of its underground *residenturas* (intelligence apparatuses in foreign countries headed by *resident directors*) abroad is to inform the Soviet government by radio and other means about the war plans of the enemy, his troop concentrations and movements, the size of the uncommitted reserves in terms of men and materiel, the extent of the damage inflicted on the enemy by the air forces of the Soviet Union and its allies. The so-called Diplomatic Intelligence concentrates the efforts of its informants and secret agents on watching the relations among the governments of the enemy coalition with special emphasis on friction among them. The Soviet *residenturas* keep a sharp eye also on Russia's allies in the war and immediately signal the Soviet government if information has been received that an ally of Russia has put out peace feelers or is gravitating toward a separate peace with the enemy. It may be recalled that during World War II, the Kremlin sounded an alarm when it intercepted rumors that British representatives were about to meet in Franco's Spain with emissaries of Hitler. During the worst days of the war, when Russia's defenses were crumbling and the Western allies were slow in opening a second front, there were moments when the Western leaders were jittery at the thought that Stalin might try to save what was left of the country by making a separate peace with Germany.

In wartime, the principal task before all the Soviet *residenturas* abroad (KGB and military) is to keep the government informed of the enemy's grand strategy and his capabilities and vulnerabilities and to furnish the Soviet High Command with data necessary to enable it to work out its own plans and strategy. The day-to-day tactical or *combat* intelligence is taken care of by the intelligence apparatuses of the Soviet armed forces and by the Special Departments (*Osoby Otdel*) of the KGB attached to all army units from regimental strength up. It is their duty to supply the Soviet commander with data on the size, disposition, and fighting strength of the enemy force with which the troops under his command will soon be locked in battle. The standard sources of military intelligence are supplemented with information obtained from enemy headquarters raided by the KGB guerrilla detachments, from ground and aerial photographic reconnaissance, from interrogated prisoners, and from refugees and spies who pose as refugees.

The third line of Soviet intelligence is the so-called *Economic Intelligence*. Contrary to the existing view, the Division of Economic Intelligence had little to do with studying the economy of foreign countries, but was created for the purpose of exercising state control over the Soviet export and import operations, and of protecting the foreign trade of the Soviet Union from the pressures and abuses of the world cartels and other organizations of monopolistic capital. Thus, for instance, the Division of Economic Intelligence discovered in the 1930's that the biggest electric concerns of the world had entered into a so-called gentlemen's agreement by which they obligated themselves not to compete with each other in dealings with Soviet Russia and to overcharge her on her purchases up to 75 per cent of the existing world prices. I have seen a letter signed by a vice-president of the General Electric Co. and addressed to the president of the AEG in Germany, Mr. Bleiman, and to the president of the Swiss Brown Bovery Co., which contained a list of prices made up especially for the Soviet Union that were from 60 to 75 per cent higher than the regular market prices. General Electric considered it necessary to justify the exorbitant prices by stating in its letter that Russia's credit standing in the world was "not too good." This gentlemen's agreement was finally broken up by the Soviet government, but not before Soviet trade had suffered huge losses which amounted to tens of millions of dollars.

The fourth line of Soviet intelligence is so-called *Misinformation*. The Soviet government is interested not only in obtaining information about the policies and impending moves of foreign governments, but also in misinforming and misleading the governments of foreign countries concerning its own position and intentions. But whereas in the field of procuring secret information from abroad the intelligence officer is given free rein to steal whatever he considers valuable to his country, the task of misinforming the outer world about the Soviet Union cannot be left to the discretion of the individual officer or even of the Soviet intelligence service as a whole. The matter of deciding what information or rumors, if any, should be deviously planted within the earshot of a certain foreign government is a question of high policy in itself and must be subordinated to the specific aims pursued by the Soviet highest policymakers. Misinformation is not just lying for the sake of lying; it is expected to serve as a subtle means of inducing another government to do what the Kremlin wants it to do or to frighten and bluff a foreign government into inaction or into making a concession to the U.S.S.R. Therefore, in the area of misinformation the Soviet intelligence cannot act without specific and clear directives of the government as to the substance of the misinformation and the manner in which it should be launched.

For instance, in the 1930's when the Soviet government sought to obtain a mutual defense treaty with France in order to counteract the growing menace of Hitler's Germany, Soviet intelligence was given instructions to introduce into the channels of the French General Staff (without showing the Soviet's hand) certain pages from a German army report which indicated that Germany was planning to occupy the Rhineland at the beginning of 1936 and to invade France within eighteen months after that. About the same time the Soviet intelligence, also on instructions of the government, tried to shake England out of her complacency by slipping into British secret channels (through a German double agent) inflated figures of German aircraft production. This created quite a stir in the highest councils of the British government. It was the task of the Misinformation desk of the KGB Intelligence Directorate to fabricate photocopies of ostensibly German documents with such skill that they would look genuine and convincing even to trained military experts.

During the Spanish Civil War, in which a Russian tank brigade fought against the forces of General Franco and Russian pilots flew the newest Soviet fighters (I-15 and I-16) and medium bombers (CB) against the German air squadrons, the Misinformation desk was ordered to introduce into the channels of the German military intelligence service information that the Soviet planes fighting in Spain were not of the latest design and that Russia had in her arsenal thousands of newer planes, of the second and third generation, possessing much greater speed and a higher ceiling. This was not true. Russia had given Spain the best and the newest she had (though in insufficient quantities). This misleading information greatly impressed the German High Command, because when in August 1937 German experts examined and tested two Soviet I-16 fighter planes which landed by mistake on an enemy air strip behind the Madrid sector they were amazed at the quality and performance of the planes, which in some respects surpassed German fighters. After this, the news that the Russians had on the production line still better and more modern models gave the Germans something to think about. Evidently, Stalin wanted to impress on Hitler that the Soviet Union was much stronger and better armed than he thought and that it would be wiser for Germany to have Russia as a partner rather than an opponent.

The fifth line of Soviet intelligence is *Infiltration of Security Agencies and Intelligence Services of Foreign Countries*. This activity contains a special challenge to Soviet intelligence officers and holds for them a peculiar kind of fascination. Although they regard foreign intelligence officers as professional spies (they think of themselves as revolutionaries carrying out dangerous assignments of the party), they do have a feeling of kinship with them and react to a suddenly encountered foreign intelligence agent with the same thrill and curiosity with which two enemy pilots sight each other over the wide spaces in the sky. The general attitude of the Soviet intelligence officer toward his foreign counterpart is hostile, but it is sincerely friendly from the moment the foreign intelligence man becomes an informant for Russia.

The principal aims which the Soviet intelligence pursues by infiltrating foreign intelligence services are:

In relation to security agencies:

To find out what the security agencies of the foreign country know about the activities of the Soviet intelligence on the territory of that country.

To find out whether these agencies have succeeded in planting their counterspies in the Soviet network or in recruiting somebody connected with the *residentura*.

To learn in good time whether the security agencies intend to arrest someone from the Soviet network.

To use the facilities of the foreign security agencies for the purpose of checking on persons in whom the Soviet *residentura* happens to be interested.

In relation to foreign intelligence services, it is important to find out:

Whether the foreign intelligence agency has succeeded in creating a spy network on the territory of Soviet Russia.

Who the spies are in Russia who betray the country to foreign intelligence services.

What secret information had been transmitted from Russia to the foreign intelligence agency.

What lines of communications exist between the secret network in Russia and the foreign intelligence services abroad (such as diplomatic pouch, tourists, and radio transmitters).

In some Western countries the intelligence services enjoy access to the confidential papers of other departments of government, including those of defense and of foreign affairs. The intelligence services justify their right of access to these confidential materials on the ground that (*a*) it helps them to evaluate information obtained from their own secret sources abroad and that (*b*) analysis of the materials from the departments of defense and of foreign affairs in conjunction with their own information from secret sources helps them to render more accurate estimates of the intentions, capabilities, and over-all strength of other countries. Whatever the merits or demerits of such an arrangement are, the Foreign Directorate of the NKVD was quick to take advantage of the convenient concentration of secret documents from various government departments in one place and instructed its *residenturas* abroad to strive to procure from the foreign intelligence services not only the data of the intelligence services themselves, but also the information which they receive from other government departments, such as reports by army, navy, and air attachés, as well as political analyses and estimates furnished by ambassadors.

The Soviet intelligence strives to penetrate the intelligence agencies of foreign states for another reason as well. Although the relations among the intelligence services of the capitalistic countries are not always harmonious, due to rivalry and personal jealousies, they do co-operate with each other to a certain extent in matters of combating Soviet espionage and subversion. Some of them exchange information on the subject and forward to each other photographs of persons known to them as Soviet spies or suspected of being such. The acquisition of this correspondence between foreign intelligence agencies is valuable to the Soviet intelligence because it reveals what is known about Russian intelligence activities and may sometimes tip off the Soviet intelligence that some of its agents are in danger of being exposed and arrested.

It must be said, however, that the secret information procured from foreign intelligence services has rarely given the Soviet intelligence cause for alarm. Much of that information was incompetent, out of date, and as a rule the strength of the Soviet armed forces was ridiculously belittled in it. The reports of the foreign intelligence services on the Soviet espionage activities were based more on hindsight than foresight and frequently contained outright fantasies concocted by unscrupulous doubles and falsifiers. However, if much of the information collected by the foreign intelligence services about Russia was found to be worthless, it was by no means worthless to the Soviet intelligence to know this.

Two basic elements are considered indispensable to enable the policymakers of a government to chart a correct foreign policy in a time of crisis. One is to know the real power of their own country. The other is to know the power of the potential enemy. But to this a third element must be added: a government must also know the *image* of its own country as reflected in the eyes of the adversary. This is very important because, even if that image is distorted, *the adversary is going to act upon it.*

By infiltrating the intelligence services of foreign countries, the Soviet intelligence is able to learn and to report to the Soviet policymakers, how various states assess the capabilities, deficiencies, and military strength of the Soviet Union. It is then the task of the Soviet policymakers to try to foresee what mistakes the potential enemies of Russia will be likely to make, when the chips are down, as a result of the distorted view they hold about the Soviet Union as a world power.

The infiltration of a foreign intelligence service is a much more hazardous operation than the acquisition of informants in other government departments, because the officers of a foreign intelligence service are aware of these things and may maneuver the recruiting Soviet agent into a trap, or seize him outright before he has a chance to retreat. That is why the Foreign Directorate of the KGB advises its *residenturas* abroad not to rush things, but before attempting to recruit a foreign intelligence officer, to approach and cultivate a friend or relative of his first and then use that friend as a go-between. The *residenturas* are advised to arrange things in such a way that the actual recruiting should be done on the territory of a neighboring state and that until the recruited officer has proved his sincerity by turning over vital information to the Russians, the meetings with him should continue to take place outside his country. However, the safest way to infiltrate a foreign intelligence service without fear of being caught in a trap is to plant a completely reliable person in that organization. Thus, for instance, an old and trusted informant who happens to be an officer in good standing in some other branch of the foreign government may be induced to seek employment with the intelligence service. Sometimes it may be necessary for him to become socially acquainted with a senior officer of the intelligence service first and thus pave the way for the appointment. Secret agents planted by the *residentura* in a foreign intelligence service can be used not only for the purpose of procuring secret information but also as a channel through which misinformation about the Soviet Union and other countries can be introduced.

It must be stated here that none of the world powers escaped the infiltration of its intelligence and security services by Soviet agents. General Walter Bedell Smith, the former head of the American C.I.A., was aware of the successes of the Soviet intelligence in this field and in September 1953 expressed his apprehension in the following words: "I believe the communists are so adroit and adept that they have infiltrated practically every security agency of the government."

The sixth line of Soviet intelligence consists of *influencing decisions of foreign governments* through secret agents in important positions within the councils of the foreign states. The history of the last two decades offers a number of examples of highly placed Soviet secret agents being able to tip the scales in the field of policymaking in favor of the Soviet Union. Some of these secret agents started out as junior diplomats in the foreign offices of the West and climbed with the help of their socially prominent families to high government positions. Others were already mature politicians and statesmen when they were seduced by money and other base considerations. One of the leading members of Mussolini's cabinet and the Fascist Grand Council succumbed to an offer of money and agreed to collaborate with Soviet Russia.

In one mid-European country, a leading member of the parliament, who was not considered a friend of the Soviet Union, would meet the Soviet ambassador secretly and receive instructions from him concerning the position to take in certain matters affecting interests of Soviet Russia. In another European country an inspector of the national secret police, who became a secret Soviet informant, reported to the Soviet *residentura* that the police were in possession of documentary proof that an influential cabinet member of the country was a partner in a big narcotics ring and that together with a famous racketeer he owned a "luxurious" brothel in the center of the capital, a few blocks away from the presidency of the republic. The minister was so powerful in the councils of the government, as well as in the underworld, that the head of the secret police was afraid to denounce him. Moscow ordered the *residentura* to steal all the incriminating documents. After that, photographs of the documents were shown to the minister at the Soviet embassy by the Soviet ambassador himself, as a "friendly gesture." This ambassador happened to be none other than the former chief of the Foreign Department of the OGPU, that is, of Soviet intelligence. The ambassador's friendly gesture was well understood and served as a prelude which opened up a period of close collaboration between the highly influential minister and the Soviet intelligence. His task was not merely to inform but to influence the policies of his government in the direction indicated by the Soviet Foreign Commissariat.

Two other functions belong to the same sixth line of activity of the KGB intelligence. One consists of paving the way for future negotiations between the Soviet Foreign Office and other governments on ticklish international matters. This is usually done by way of exploratory talks conducted by Soviet intelligence agents, through go-betweens or directly, with representatives of a foreign government. If the talks produce results satisfactory to both sides, the official diplomats of both countries take over. These exploratory talks were resorted to in cases in which the Kremlin wanted to be free to disclaim any knowledge of them. One Russian intelligence officer by the name of Ostrovsky, who had secretly negotiated the establishment of diplomatic relations with Romania, became the first Soviet ambassador to that country.

Another function along the same line of intelligence activity consisted of clandestine attempts to induce leaders of the political opposition in a foreign country to stage a *coup d'état* and take over the government. In such cases the Soviet government held out a promise of political and financial support and, if that particular state happened to be adjacent to the territory of the Soviet Union, military aid as well. Thus, in 1937, one of the chiefs of the KGB intelligence was commissioned by Stalin personally to enter into secret negotiations with former Romanian Minister of Foreign Affairs Titulescu, who lived at that time in Menton, on the Franco-Italian border, and persuade him to overthrow the reactionary regime of Prime Minister Maniu. Stalin

offered financial and military aid against a promise
by Titulescu that upon assumption of power he would
sign a mutual assistance pact with the Soviet Union.

The seventh line of the Soviet intelligence is the so-
called *Industrial Intelligence*. Although intelligence as
such has been known for hundreds of years, this was
something new and was first initiated by the Soviets in
1929. Its purpose was to assist in the industrialization
of the Soviet Union by stealing production secrets—
new inventions, secret technological processes, etc.—
from the advanced countries of Europe and America.
With this assignment in mind the Soviet intelligence
organizations abroad began to recruit into their network engineers, scientists, and inventors working in the
laboratories and plants of the largest industrial concerns in the world. Striving to fulfill the five-year plans
of industrialization, the Soviets were buying quantities
of machinery and even whole plants from industrial
companies in the West. At the same time they conducted negotiations with these companies for the purchase of patents and the know-how processes of production. A number of these were purchased, and
foreign engineers began to arrive in Russia to instruct
and train the Russians in the application of the new
methods.

But often, when the price demanded by foreign concerns for their so-called "technical aid" was too high
—it always ran into many millions of dollars—the head
of the Soviet government would challenge the Foreign
Department of the NKVD to steal the secret inventions
from the Western companies. The response of the Foreign Department of the NKVD to these challenges was
invariably enthusiastic, and after a number of success-

fully accomplished missions, the government created within the Foreign Department of the NKVD a new Division for Industrial Intelligence.

Sometimes, the theft of all the necessary formulas, blueprints, and instructions was insufficient to enable the Soviet engineers and inventors to reconstruct a complicated mechanism or to duplicate a production process. Something would be missing, and this *something* was the human element, the special skill and engineering instinct. In such cases officers of the Division for Industrial Intelligence would press the foreign engineers, with offers of additional rewards, to make a secret trip to Russia for a short time to instruct the Russian engineers and supervise the laboratory experiments on the spot. Preparing the trip, the Soviet *residentura* would take special precautions to insure that the passport of the traveler should not bear any border stamps and other traces of his visit to the Soviet Union. With this in mind, the engineer would apply for a passport and with it travel to the capital of an adjacent country. There he would turn his passport over to the local Soviet agent for safekeeping and get from him a false one on which he would proceed to Russia. On his return trip he would pick up his genuine passport where he had left it, turn in the false one, and continue homeward. The fees paid by the Russians for such trips ran sometimes as high as $10,000 for a few days' work, but the savings to the Soviets amounted to millions. The following illustrates how the Division of Industrial Intelligence worked in one of its standard operations.

As the Soviet Union was spending huge sums of money on industrial diamonds needed for the expanding oil industry, metallurgy, and various geological projects, the Soviet government became interested in an offer made by the German Krupp concern to supply Russia with newly invented artificial diamonds which were almost as hard and good as natural ones. The new product was named *"widi,"* an abbreviation of *wie diamant,* which in German means "like diamond." The Soviet Commissariat of Heavy Industry bought some of the *widi* diamonds, tested them in drilling operations, and was amazed at their high quality. The commissariat decided to buy the patent for the production of *widi* from Krupp and have the German engineers build a plant in the Soviet Union. Soon a delegation of German experts headed by two Krupp directors arrived in Moscow. They knew how badly the Russians needed industrial diamonds for the five-year plan of industrialization and demanded a staggering price for the technical aid which Russia wanted.

When the deal was being discussed at the Politburo, Stalin turned to the head of the NKVD and said: "The bastards want too much money. Try to steal it from them. Show what the NKVD can do!" This was a challenge. One of the chiefs of the Foreign Department was charged with this operation. Before tackling the difficult assignment, it was necessary first to find out the location of the *widi*-producing plant and the names of the inventor and the engineers in charge of production. This task was assigned to a German scientist, Dr. B., who was a Soviet secret agent. Dr. B. looked up in the Berlin Technische Hochschule, with which he was associated, all the available data on the methods of achieving hard metal alloys and approached a noted professor who had written treatises on the subject. From him Dr. B. learned that a Krupp inventor had succeeded in attaining the hardest alloy known and that it was being produced in a plant on the outskirts of Berlin. Dr. B. visited the site of the plant and dropped in at a beer hall where the technical personnel drank their beer. He visited the place a few times and engaged some of the technicians in conversations. Dr. B. represented himself as a scientist who was writing a book on hard-metal alloys. "Oh, then you are working with our Cornelius," said one technician. Dr. B. pricked up his ears, but said that he was not and remarked that he had known a Professor Cornelius. "No," said the technician, "he is not a professor, he is only a foreman in our plant, but he is a man who could teach the professors how to make industrial diamonds." Through an inspector of the Berlin Polizei Presidium, who was a secret Soviet informant, the Russian *residentura* obtained general information on Cornelius and his home address.

Next day, Dr. B. rang the doorbell of Cornelius' home. He was admitted by the wife of Cornelius. She told him that her husband had not yet returned from the plant, a fact which was known to Dr. B. He had come earlier on purpose, hoping that while waiting for Cornelius he might learn something about him from his wife. Dr. B. told her that he was a doctor of science who was writing a treatise on hard-metal alloys and that his colleagues from the Technische Hochschule advised him to see Mr. Cornelius, who might be helpful to him. He added that if Mr. Cornelius was really an expert in that field, he might earn some money on the side, if he were willing to contribute to the research. The wife of Cornelius felt very flattered that a scientist from the famous Technische Hochschule should come to seek advice of her husband. The prospect of earning extra money was also stimulating. She began to praise her husband's abilities and high reputation at the plant. She said that the engineer who had invented the process of artificial diamonds trusted only her husband, because he alone knew how to handle the specially built electric oven, and that now, after the inventor had fallen out with the Krupps and quit, her husband was practically in charge of the whole thing. He could demand any salary he wanted from Krupp, and they would have to give it to him; but he is not that kind of a man . . . To him devotion to the company came first!

Soon Cornelius returned home. Dr. B. stated to him his problem, and in order to underscore his purely scientific interest in the matter and allay any possible suspicion, he invited Cornelius to his personal room at the Technische Hochschule for the coming Saturday. From the Technische Hochschule, Dr. B. took Cornelius for dinner to his luxurious ten-room flat in the eight-story apartment house which Dr. B. had inherited from his father.

Dr. B. saw at once that Cornelius was too illiterate technologically to be able to explain in scientific terms the secret of production, even if he wanted to. He was only a foreman who had been trained by the inventor to operate the oven. What Dr. B. wanted was to find out the name of the inventor, his whereabouts, and the history of his break with the Krupp concern. Dr. B. was very intelligent and knew how to stimulate a conversation and make a man talk. After an excellent dinner and a few glasses of strong brandy, Cornelius did not mind telling the story to his friendly host.

The inventor's name was Mr. Worm. When Worm saw at what fabulous prices Krupp was selling the industrial diamonds which he had created and which cost the company so little, he decided to build his own shop secretly and then compete with Krupp. He rented a little shop, made an oven like the one he had constructed for Krupp, installed the minimum of equipment needed, and made a few profitable sales of the *widi* diamonds to foreign customers. With the money received he paid off some of the loans he got from the bank for launching his enterprise. Worm was on the way to becoming a rich man, but the Krupp concern soon learned about his disloyal competition and swooped down on him with all the fury of an industrial giant. Worm was summarily fired. His customers were warned that if they bought a single ounce of *widi* from him, Krupp would never sell them anything. The banks suddenly became rigid and demanded prompt payment from Worm, who, in spite of his talents as an engineer and inventor, could not find work. All the doors were politely but firmly closed in his face.

Dr. B. hurried to see Mr. Worm. Here, too, he managed to ring the doorbell when Worm was not at home. Dr. B. found that women were less secretive and more talkative than men, especially when they had an opportunity to do a bit of advertising for their husbands. Mr. Worm's wife was happy to hear that somebody had become interested in her husband. She must have been desperate enough to tell her husband's story to a complete stranger. The Krupps were brutes, she complained. They ruled the country. Her husband was a martyr. They had driven him to desperation. All his savings had gone into the enterprise, and it was ruined with one blow. Dr. B. listened to her story with unfeigned sympathy. He said that he had an interesting proposition for her husband which might get him out of his difficulties. From that moment on Mrs. Worm became his trusting friend. She believed this man would find a way to save her husband from the strangling power of the Krupps. Because Worm was slow in coming, Dr. B. left without seeing him. He asked to have Worm call him up. Next day they met at the Technische Hochschule, and from there they went to Dr. B's apartment. Dr. B. told Worm that he knew about his difficulties and that if he wished to escape from the stranglehold of the Krupps, he must offer his talents to a foreign concern. Dr. B. said he knew a big Scandinavian company which might be interested in acquiring the secret process of *widi* production and in entering the field in competition with Krupp. A few days later, Dr. B. informed Worm that the company was definitely interested in the project and had authorized him to advance to Worm up to ten thousand German marks. He asked Worm to submit a statement on the *widi* production process and to furnish data about the equipment needed, its cost, etc. For the time being, Dr. B. declined to name the company. This did not necessarily look suspicious, because Dr. B., as a go-between, was entitled to a commission and might have been protecting his own interests. However, Worm got a strange hunch. "I want to warn you," said he to Dr. B., "that if my invention is needed for the Russians, I will have nothing to do with them!" Dr. B. was taken aback, but hastened to reassure him that it was a Scandinavian concern all right. As it has turned out, Worm was a fanatical Nazi and a Russian hater.

Something had to be done to placate that burning hatred if Worm was to be maneuvered into giving his *widi* invention to Russia. While Worm was writing the report, Dr. B. would raise the advance and add to it a thousand marks every week or so, which delighted Mrs. Worm. In the meantime Dr. B. had Worm and his wife a few times for dinner at his home and tried to ingratiate himself with the lady. Mrs. Worm started to buy things which she had long been denying herself, while her husband kept a wary eye on his dwindling advance. Dr. B. noticed this and immediately came to her assistance. He began to give her money in secret from Worm with the understanding that she would repay it when her husband struck it rich. Dr. B. was convinced that a prosperous future awaited Worm just around the corner.

Meanwhile, the account submitted by Worm was sent to Moscow. After a close study the Russian engineers declared that without the personal guidance of the inventor they would not be able to construct the special oven, which was supposed to make several thousand revolutions a minute under an enormously high temperature. Moscow wanted to have the inventor at all cost. And so Dr. B's friendship with Worm's wife paid off. She cajoled her husband for a week until she brought him to realize that they had no choice and that this was their last and only chance. The Soviet trade delegation in Berlin signed an official two-year contract with Worm, according to which he received a certain sum in German currency, a salary for himself in Russian rubles, and a monthly allowance in German marks for his wife, who preferred to remain in Germany. Worm was entitled to a suite in a first-class Moscow hotel, with restaurant and other services and also to a chauffeured automobile and to two vacations in Germany a year at Russia's expense. He took with him to Moscow a German engineer by the name of Mente who had been his assistant at the Krupp plant. Worm's letters to his wife breathed hatred toward everything Russian. He contracted rheumatic fever there and returned to Germany a disappointed and broken man. But he fulfilled his contract with the Soviets to the letter and gave them his most cherished invention.

The Division of Industrial Intelligence of the NKVD regarded the recruited foreign engineers, scientists, and inventors as its potential reserve of outstanding experts on whose collaboration the Soviet Union could count in time of war. And, indeed, when World War II broke out, most of these engineers and inventors were mobilized or integrated into the war effort in their respective countries together with the laboratories and plants where they worked. Many of them, especially those in the United States and Great Britain, were entrusted with the most sensitive projects on which the very outcome of the war depended. No wonder that the Soviet Union was in a position to know about, and often to help itself to, the newest achievements attained in the field of armaments in the leading industrial countries. The thefts of the greatest inventions of our times by the Soviet intelligence are now a matter of record, and some of the foreign scientists and engineers, such as Harry Gold, Dr. Klaus Fuchs, and Allan Nunn May, have been exposed as Soviet agents.

The eighth line of activity of the KGB intelligence is concerned with sabotage and guerrilla warfare and will be discussed in a later chapter.

III. The Illegal *Residentura* and the New Identity

The Foreign Directorate of the KGB, as well as the Intelligence Department of the Soviet Army, maintains two distinct types of intelligence organizations in foreign countries. One is called "legal *residentura*" and the other "illegal *residentura*." Both are engaged in espionage activities directed against the foreign states in which they operate, and thus their work is equally illegal as far as the laws of the foreign countries are concerned. The reason why one type has come to be called, or rather misnamed, "legal" stems from the simple fact that the Soviet intelligence officers who direct the work of the *residentura* reside in the foreign country legally, as members of the staff of the Soviet embassy or of another official Soviet agency. On the other hand, if the *residentura* is directed by Soviet intelligence officers who conceal the fact that they are Russians and reside in the foreign country with forged papers, it is called "illegal."

Until the late 1920's, the Soviet intelligence operations abroad were directed from the Soviet embassies exclusively. During that period the "legal" *residenturas* accomplished a lot of highly successful work. However, one aspect of these *residenturas* troubled the Soviet government. Each time a spy ring working for the Soviets was exposed, the trail led straight to the Soviet embassy with all the resulting adverse publicity. And when some of the arrested spies turned out to be communists, the press would raise a bitter campaign against the local Communist party, branding it as a gang of Soviet spies masquerading as a legitimate political party. What the Soviet government wanted was to reorganize its intelligence operations on foreign soil in such a manner that if some of its agents were caught, the trail would not lead to the Soviet embassy, and the Soviet government would be able to disclaim any connection with the exposed spy ring.

The answer to this dilemma was the creation of the so-called "illegal *residentura*." The principal new feature of that intelligence apparatus consisted in the fact that it was completely divorced from the Soviet embassy and operated in the underground from top to bottom. The Soviet intelligence officers in charge of the secret network no longer enjoyed the immunity of the Soviet embassy and the privileges of the diplomatic Soviet passport, or the facilities of the diplomatic pouch in which the stolen foreign secrets could be easily channeled to Moscow. The Soviet officers went "underground," disguised as businessmen or people of other professions, concealing their Russian nationality and hiding their identity under the cover of false foreign passports and other tricky devices. Gone was the assurance of the officer that if caught the Soviet government would launch a vigorous protest and fight for his release.

It must be noted here that, although the underground *residenturas* gradually took over the major part of the intelligence activities abroad, the legal *residenturas* were not abolished. When it came to that, the chiefs of Soviet intelligence had a change of heart and decided that it would be advantageous to Soviet intelligence to observe the international scene through two independent sets of agents and check the information supplied by one against the data received from the other. The underground *residenturas* were given broad discretional powers and an extensive scope of activities. On the other hand, the tasks of the legal *residenturas* were reduced to the most essential problems, and the residents were ordered to abstain from too risky operations that might involve the prestige of the Soviet Union. Thus, the Soviet intelligence services (of the KGB and of the army) retained a dual system of *residenturas,* the so-called "legal" and "illegal."

The transition of the Soviet intelligence to underground methods of operation was not easy. The difficulty lay in the fact that there were not many intelligence officers who knew languages well enough to be able to pass for nationals of foreign countries. To overcome this difficulty a vigorous training program had been introduced. To qualify for a foreign assignment in the underground, the officer had to meet a number of requirements: (1) He had to have previous experience in intelligence and counterintelligence. (2) He had to acquire a working knowledge of the language of the country of his proposed assignment and to master the language of the country of which he would represent himself to be citizen. (3) Inasmuch as the officer was obliged to conceal his real past, he had to contrive and prepare for himself a new and sound life story which could withstand at least superficial investigation. (4) He had to acquire a legitimate occupation or business cover which would justify in the eyes of the authorities his protracted sojourn in their country. The duty of the passport desk of the Foreign Department of the KGB was to provide the officer with a genuine-looking foreign passport that would blend with his personal characteristics and to instruct him on various technicalities connected with its use.

The passport of a person is an important part of his identity, and for that reason all intelligence services take pains to provide their undercover agents with the best passports possible, the forgery of which would be difficult to uncover. When the NKVD intelligence had just begun to build its underground network in a number of countries, it resorted to two methods of obtaining foreign passports for its operatives. One consisted of using a genuine passport of a foreigner who had immigrated to the Soviet Union and substituting the photograph of the operative for the photograph of the former bearer. However, this method was not considered safe enough because a close examination of the passport by experts under a proper lamp would have disclosed that the photograph had been changed. The second method consisted of the outright fabrication of foreign passports by highly skilled experts at the Soviet government engraving offices. These passports were so perfect that even experienced engravers were unable to distinguish them from genuine ones. But they had one inherent weakness. In case the bearer of the passport fell under the suspicion of the police, it was enough for them to make an inquiry at the passport office of the country which had allegedly made out the passport, and they would be informed that such a passport, in the name of so and so, had never been issued.

In view of the defectiveness of both methods, the NKVD intelligence began to look for a more satisfactory solution of the problem. All Soviet *residenturas* abroad were instructed to explore in great detail the procedure of the issuance of passports in various countries of Europe and America, and when all the gathered data was studied in Moscow, the intelligence chiefs came to the conclusion that with the proper application of a certain amount of fraud their agents could acquire genuine passports direct from government passport offices in the same way that citizens of those countries did. All the Soviet intelligence officer had to do was to pretend to be a citizen of the country, furnish corroborating proof to that effect, and apply for a travel passport.

The first attempts of this kind proved very successful, and soon Soviet agents began to show each other with pride their genuine passports with their own photographs affixed to them. The most popular passport among Soviet intelligence officers was that of the United States. And no wonder. The American passport carried with it the prestige of a great power, and the police agencies of Europe and Asia did not dare, at least in those times, to arrest or search an American citizen with the same want of consideration and recklessness which they were prone to display toward a citizen of Romania, Bulgaria, Finland, or Honduras. The American passport afforded still another advantage: with it a traveler could go to many countries without the need to apply for an entrance visa. But the main advantage of the American passport lay in the fact that its bearer was not obliged to speak perfect English because the United States has millions of naturalized citizens who had come from tsarist Russia and whose English is far from perfect, and is often outright poor.

In the United States the Soviet agents obtain passports by various artifices, of which I shall mention two:

(1) The intelligence agent acquires naturalization papers belonging to a Russian immigrant; pretending that they are his own he presents them to a local branch of the Passport Division of the State Department, fills out the proper application form, and requests that a passport be issued to him for foreign travel. He swears to the truthfulness of the information furnished in the application and invites two witnesses to verify his identity under oath.

It goes without saying that when the intelligence agent selects naturalization papers for himself he must see to it that the age and other personal data which they contain should coincide with his own. How careful one must be with these things, one can judge from the following episode. In 1930 a Soviet intelligence agent who was thirty years old acquired somebody's naturalization papers and was about to present them to the Passport Division with his application. While he talked things over with the men who were going to accompany him to the government office as witnesses, one of them noticed that the year of birth entered in the naturalization certificate was 1877, which would make the applicant fifty-three years old. The intelligence officer was greatly surprised. To him the figure 1877 looked like 1899, because the Americans inscribe the digit "7" exactly as the Russians write "9."

The officer who has acquired an American passport through fraud does not feel completely safe as long as his double, the real owner of the naturalization papers, continues to live in the United States. For that reason, the Russians try to persuade Americans whose papers have been fraudulently used, to immigrate to Russia, where they are given jobs and financial aid.

(2) The Soviet intelligence agents obtain American

passports also by the following ruse: they examine birth and death records in the archives of the department of health and take down the data of the birth and death of a male child many years back. If the date of birth is more or less that of the intelligence officer and he likes the name and place of birth, he obtains for a nominal fee a photostat of the birth entry. Claiming it as his own, the agent applies on the basis of the photostat for a passport. Two witnesses confirm under oath that they had known the applicant for at least five years and they certify his identity.

To pose at the Division of Passports as a born American, the intelligence agent must, of course, speak English well enough not to arouse the suspicion of the government clerk. But in cases when the clerk had been bribed, the inadequacy of the applicant's English does not matter. Later, in his future associations with other Americans, the intelligence officer can explain away his foreign accent by telling them that when he was still a child his parents took him to another country where he was brought up and that later he returned to the United States and claimed citizenship, to which he was entitled by virtue of birth.

The United States is not the only country where the Russian agents acquire passports by false pretenses. In every large country the Soviet intelligence finds loopholes in the existing passport regulations through which it obtains genuine passports for its undercover agents. In some countries the Soviet intelligence keeps on its payroll clerks from government passport bureaus.

Soviet women, who work in the underground *residenturas,* acquire foreign passports by the same means as do men. But they have at their disposal an even better way, which can never be exposed—marriage, fictitious marriage, of course. According to the laws of a number of countries, as in England for instance, foreign women who marry nationals of those countries automatically acquire the citizenship of their husbands. One Soviet woman who needed a British passport to take up her assignment in Japan told me that when she married an Englishman and applied in London for a British passport, the government clerk explained to her that it would take about two weeks, but that if she wanted to get the passport sooner she might have it in one or two days on the payment of a nominal fee. She did so and got her passport the next day.

Fictitious marriages became a fashionable phenomenon in the 1930's. Owing to the growth of anti-Fascist sentiments among university students, especially in Great Britain and the United States, many young men, mostly from wealthy and aristocratic families, lent themselves to the role of fictitious husbands *for the cause*. Some kept such marriages secret from their families, but others brought their wives home to the consternation of their parents. Only rarely have the fictitious marriages evolved into genuine ones; in most cases the husband and bride drifted apart without even the benefit of a proper honeymoon. A few of these women married sons of millionaires, but I have yet to hear that one of them has tried to get a portion of her rich husband's estate in a divorce suit.

The Soviet intelligence used to obtain passports also from a few foreign consuls who were on the Soviet payroll, and there were instances when they intervened energetically in behalf of their "citizens" when these got in trouble with the security authorities. I remember a case when D. Smirnov, a former secretary of the Soviet embassy in Paris, was detained by the Polish border police when he was passing through Poland on the way to the Soviet Union with a Greek passport. The reason for his detention was that two Polish police officers recognized Smirnov as the man who a year before had traveled from the Soviet Union to France, through Poland, with a Soviet diplomatic passport. To make things worse our Greek traveler could not say a single word in Greek. However, the Greek consul in Danzig who had supplied Smirnov with the passport rushed personally to his defense and insisted that the bearer of the passport was Greek. He agreed to certify this in writing. The Poles, evidently, had some regard for the consul (or may be he was supplying them with passports too), and Smirnov was released with an apology delivered in pure Russian.

No matter how good the passport acquired by the agent may be, a skillful investigation will sooner or later establish that its bearer is not its lawful owner. A false passport serves the intelligence agent well only till the day when he has fallen under the surveillance of the authorities. It also affords the agent a breathing spell (while the document is being checked) during which he may escape.

It must be understood that a man is physically unable to assume the traits and characteristics of another man to such an extent that people would not be able to distinguish him from the man whom he tries to impersonate. In our civilized society the past of a man leaves indelible traces, and various phases of this past can be verified. Let us assume that a Soviet operative has succeeded in misrepresenting the naturalization papers of a Russian immigrant, Peter Gorin, as his own and in acquiring for himself an American passport in

that name. Let us also assume that the personal characteristics of the Soviet agent (age, height, and other
traits) jibe completely with those of Gorin. Let us also
suppose that the real Gorin has been persuaded to go
to Russia, leaving the Soviet agent as the only Gorin
as far as the naturalization papers and passport are
concerned. But in spite of all that, it would be enough
for the police authorities to dig a little deeper and the
forgery would inevitably come to light.

The authorities would have only to show Gorin's
passport photograph to those who had attended school
with him or had worked with him to find that this was
not the picture of the Gorin they had known. It would
be enough to compare the handwriting of the suspected
Gorin with that of the real one (his school papers, ap-
plications for social security, or life insurance) and
the masquerade would be over.

However, thanks to its constant striving toward per-
fection, the Soviet intelligence has in many cases succeeded in contriving such artful ruses as have lent an
almost indestructible authenticity to the concocted
identity of the agent and made it impervious to exposure. How this was done can be seen from the following examples.

In the Foreign Department of the NKVD there
served an intelligence officer by the name of Alexander
Karin, known as the man who had recruited and trained
the famous Soviet agent Richard Sorge who created a
fabulous network of spies in Japan and succeeded in
warning the Soviet government of the exact date when
the German armies would invade the Soviet Union.
Karin was an able operative and had worked abroad
with a Latvian and later with an Austrian passport, but

he did not know a single foreign language well enough to justify his continued service in the underground under the cover of a false passport. Being an ambitious operative, Karin did not want to quit the venturesome underground.

One day, a bright idea occurred to the chief of the Foreign Department of the NKVD, Artouzov, who was a friend of Karin. Artouzov had lived in Switzerland before the Russian Revolution. He had known a well-to-do couple there, whose daughter went on a trip to Russia at the beginning of the century, and had met and married a young Russian teacher. In 1903 she gave birth to a boy. When the child was seven, his mother died. The grandparents in Switzerland showed great concern for their grandson and were in constant correspondence with his father.

When in 1917 the country was swept by the Revolution and civil war accompanied by mass migration of the population, the old people lost track of their grandson. The letters they wrote to Russia remained unanswered. Artouzov sized up this drama and suggested that Karin impersonate the grandson, enter into correspondence with the family of "his" late mother, and express a desire to emigrate to Switzerland. Meanwhile, the grandfather died, but the old lady was still alive. Her two sons were wealthy businessmen with respectable positions in Swiss society. In accord with Artouzov's plan, a touching correspondence sprang up between the grandson (Karin) and his grandmother. He sent her the old photographs and letters of his "poor mother," and hinted that he would like to emigrate to Switzerland if this were possible. The Swiss family at once mobilized all its connections among the diplomatic and business circles in Europe inviting them to use their influence with the Soviet authorities and persuade them to allow the young man to leave Russia.

The Soviet authorities, that is, Artouzov himself, proved sympathetic toward the Swiss family and granted an exit visa to the young man, his wife, and little daughter. Karin was greatly depressed by the ignominious role he played and the warmth with which he was received by the Swiss family. The experience proved too great for the frail old lady. She died a couple of months later, happy in the belief that God had heard her prayers and fulfilled her cherished wish to see her grandson before she died. She bequeathed to Karin her house and a little estate, and soon, thanks to the un-flagging solicitude of his uncles, Karin obtained a gen-uine Swiss passport, the authenticity of which no au-thorities would be able to dispute.

Another example of the inexhaustible inventiveness of the Soviet intelligence can be drawn from a more recent event. In 1927 a Finnish immigrant in the United States, who apparently was not doing too well in this country, decided to return to Finland with his Amer-ican-born wife and son Eugene. The boy, Eugene Maki, was then eight years old.

Many years later, in 1951, a man of about thirty, entered the American legation in Helsinki, Finland, produced his American birth certificate issued by the state of Idaho in the name of Eugene Maki and said he wished to return to the United States with his young Finnish wife. As a born American, Maki was entitled to this, and a year later he was issued an American passport and left for the United States.

Everything in this episode was perfectly normal, ex-cept for one thing: the man who presented himself as

Eugene Maki, born in Enaville, Idaho, in 1919, was not Maki at all, but a Soviet KGB intelligence agent who was assigned to do espionage work in the United States. No investigative authorities in the world, no matter how clever, would be able to uncover the fraud and break the ironclad identity so masterfully created by the intelligence service for its agent, and this story would have never been revealed had not "Eugene Maki" himself, after four years of espionage activities in this country, suddenly decided to break with the Soviet Union and expose the Russian espionage activities in the United States. The real name of the man who posed as Eugene Maki is Reino Hayhanen, whose revelations culminated in the arrest and sensational trial of Colonel Rudolph Abel, who was Hayhanen's immediate superior.

IV. Departure from Moscow

When an underground operative leaves Moscow to take up his assignment in a foreign country, he does not travel from Moscow direct to his destination on his false foreign passport, because, if he did so, his passport would be stamped at the point of exit by the Soviet border guards and also by the border police of the adjacent country. These stamps would at the outset mark the bearer of the passport as a man who had something to do with communist Russia.

For that reason, the false passport is sent from Moscow by diplomatic pouch to some European capital, where it is to be picked up by the underground operative. The operative himself travels to that capital either on a Soviet passport or with a "temporary" foreign passport which is not considered safe enough for permanent use.

Having arrived in the country where his passport awaits him, the operative undergoes a complete metamorphosis. He sheds his old identity, leaving all possible traces behind, takes his false passport, and becomes an entirely new person. From there he starts to "swim," as the Soviet lingo goes, and travels to the country of his assignment.

When picking up his false passport, the operative must check whether the laboratory of the Soviet intelligence has stamped the passport with the necessary foreign exit and entry stamps to indicate the route which the passport has traveled from the country where it had been issued, because a lack of such stamps would make the border police at the next frontier crossing wonder how a person could arrive, for instance from Canada, without having had his passport stamped first at the point of exit from that country and then at the point of entry into Europe.

The quick trip of the underground operative from Moscow to the country where his false passport awaits him is considered a trifling operation and is usually prepared so carelessly that it sometimes causes the traveler trouble. Here are a few illustrations:

An officer of the NKVD intelligence, who for the first time in his career was assigned to underground work, was supposed to pass in Italy as an Austrian citizen. His false Austrian passport waited for him in Paris. For the trip from Russia to Paris he was given a "temporary" Romanian passport. He traveled from the Black Sea port of Odessa to Istanbul, and there boarded a Greek steamer bound for Marseilles. The journey to Turkey was uneventful enough. But on the boat to Marseilles he was suddenly seized with excruciating pain in the abdomen. The boat physician, a Greek, hurried to his aid. He tried to talk to him first in Greek and then in English, but the patient did not understand either of the languages.

As good luck would have it, the purser of the boat located a Romanian passenger and asked him to act as an interpreter. This passenger turned out to be the Romanian consul general in France. But to everybody's surprise, the patient could not understand a single word of his "native" tongue. The situation was becoming critical as the Greek physician was trying to explain to the patient in sign language that he considered it necessary to operate on him for appendicitis . . .

Another case concerned an underground operative who had to get away from Hitler's Germany in a hurry. He hid his false Canadian passport, in which he figured as an exporter, and asked the NKVD secret laboratory in Germany to give him a "temporary" passport for a quick trip to Russia. The laboratory hastily fixed a Portuguese passport for him. When he arrived in Moscow, a friend of his who had worked in Portugal took a look at the passport and said: "It's your luck that the German and Polish border police did not know Portuguese. It is written here that the bearer of the passport has only one arm."

Still another incident which bordered on the comic was related to me by an underground resident named Karl, who operated in France with a Czechoslovakian passport. He left Paris for Moscow using a temporary American passport. When the train came to the Belgian frontier, an officer entered the compartment to check the documents. Karl produced his American passport and it was duly stamped. Simultaneously, the only other passenger in the compartment, a neat middle-aged gentleman with silvery hair produced his passport—he also was an American! From that moment the man became Karl's tormentor. He was happy to meet a compatriot, and soon he was telling about his wonderful trip to Italy and Spain and plying Karl with questions. Was he also on a pleasure trip, or on business? When did he leave the United States? Where was he going? Soon the man took out his wallet and produced snapshots of his grandchildren. Karl, who did not speak English and knew only a few stock phrases, became morose and taciturn. He answered "yes" and "no," not knowing to what he was answering. To get rid of the friendly old man, Karl pretended to doze off, but it was enough for him to open his eyes and the man was again upon him.

After a while, Karl took out a French magazine and pretended to be absorbed in reading. But the man was looking at him and waiting for an opening . . . Karl left the compartment, went to another car, and sat there for an hour. Then he went to the dining car for dinner. He was very hungry and started to relish his soup. At that moment the American appeared. And, although there were other seats in the car, the waiter chose to escort him to Karl's table. And again, indiscriminate talk and insistent questions. Karl was suffocating . . . He hurriedly swallowed a few pieces of meat, declined dessert and coffee, and left the car, still hungry. When the train pulled into the Berlin station, Karl asked the conductor to be transferred to another compartment. He saw the American again at the Russian frontier talking to other tourists. Disgusted with the journey, Karl was happy when the train finally pulled into the Moscow railway station.

Next morning, Karl came to the headquarters to report to the chief of the NKVD intelligence, Sloutsky. The secretary said that the chief had a visitor, but that Karl was welcome to enter. Karl entered, and there opposite Sloutsky with his back to the door sat a familiar figure with silvery hair. It was his tormentor! Sloutsky introduced them. The man was an old secret agent.

All these unpleasant moments that occur as a result of carelessness during the short trips with "temporary" passports are nothing in comparison with the trouble that is bound to come if similar negligence is allowed to take place on the territory of the country against which the operative conducts his dangerous work. There, the slightest misstep may mean arrest, imprisonment, and trouble for the network.

V. The Operative's Biography

The passport is only one of the components of the problem of establishing a new identity for the underground operative. Like any other person, the operative must have a "past," his own history, capable of withstanding at least a superficial investigation. The best way to acquire a past is to build it around the life story of the man whose passport has been taken and whose double he has become. However, this must not be done blindly, but in a very careful and selective way.

Let us assume that the man who has relinquished his passport to the operative is an American, that his parents reside in New York, and that he had been with General Motors for a number of years. It is clear that if the parents of this man are not privy to the passport arrangement and cannot be relied upon to confirm that the operative is their son, then it is better for the operative to say that his parents are deceased. For the same reason, it would be a mistake for the operative to indicate General Motors as the place of his former employment, because, in case of an investigation, the other employees would not recognize in him a man who had been a co-worker. The best thing, therefore, would be for the Soviet intelligence to find a reliable businessman who would be ready to confirm that the operative had been working for him. For the same reason, it would be wrong for the operative to give the addresses at which the American had lived in the United States, as his own. What he must do is to have one or two landlords who could be relied on to confirm that at certain specified periods the operative had been their tenant. In addition to this the operative may prepare a couple of addresses of apartment houses which have been demolished.

If the operative's occupation is given in his passport, he must be able to maintain at least a general conversation about it, using the correct terms of his trade as a specialist might.

The operative must have a fair knowledge of the cities he is supposed to have lived in and of their principal attractions. If, according to the legend, he is supposed to have lived in New York, he should know the names of the boroughs, the principal buildings, avenues, parks, railway stations, bridges, department stores, theaters, subway lines, names of suburbs, etc. Before embarking on an assignment in the underground with a new passport, the operative must be given an opportunity to visit his "native" city and study it.

The operative must keep in mind that if he has fallen under the surveillance of the security agencies, it is best for him to withdraw from the field because, with rare exceptions, a thorough investigation will almost surely puncture his false identity, no matter how well it is camouflaged.

The early history of the Soviet underground was replete with incidents in which operatives discredited themselves because of lack of proper preparation. One of them, who was posing as an American, made a down payment on a little business which he bought in France, only to be confronted a few days later by a brother of the owner, an American Jew who came on a visit from New York. After a short chat with the operative in English, the American told him: "You say you are an American and that you lived in New York for some twenty years. Well, it's none of my business . . . If you want to call yourself an American, you may do so, but nobody will believe it. Please, don't be offended." The operative decided to withdraw and lost the down payment.

I remember an incident which occurred with a very able officer of the NKVD intelligence who had just arrived in France from the United States with a fresh American passport and was eager to plunge into his first venture in the underground. He stopped at the Grand Hotel in Paris, asked in fluent French for a room, and produced his American passport. The room clerk happened to be an American from Brooklyn; he was glad to welcome a compatriot in English and asked him a question or two about the crossing. Taken by surprise the Soviet officer became confused, uttered a nondescript English sentence which the clerk could not understand. He decided then to show that his English was not so bad after all and got entangled in a difficult phrase, stuttered, and went to his room, only to leave the hotel next morning. He came to the Soviet embassy utterly disappointed, deposited his American passport, and got back his Soviet documents. He wrote to Moscow that he felt he was not yet ready with the language and asked permission to go to London for three months to study English.

Another incident, also reflecting insufficient preparation for the job, took place on an ocean liner during a crossing from the United States to Europe. While playing cards with a group of passengers, a Soviet underground operative who pretended to be an American was asked what his occupation was. "A furrier," he blurted out. Had he said he was a bookseller or a dealer in fertilizers, he would have been all right. But to mention furs in the presence of women was a hazard. The ladies became very interested and began to ask him about the prices on various grades of mink and some other furs. Undaunted, the operative cited a few figures which made the ladies' eyes pop out. After that, they began to avoid him and no longer invited him to a game of cards. They eyed him suspiciously and probably thought that he was a thief or a crackpot.

Another officer, a novice in underground intelligence, made his debut on a boat from Constantinople to Marseilles. He traveled on a "temporary" Greek passport to France, where he had to pick up his permanent Austrian passport with which he was to operate in the underground. This man was also asked what his occupation was. "An exporter," he answered with a sense of importance. "Exporter of what?" was the next question. "Coffee," answered the operative. "From where?"—"From Turkey," answered the intelligence wizard. "I know," retorted the man, "that people drink coffee prepared in the Turkish fashion, but I have never heard that coffee grows in Turkey." The passengers looked at each other in amazement.

One Soviet agent who fell under the surveillance of the German police, eluded his trailers, grabbed a little suitcase, and went to a residential hotel for the week end to await an emergency passport with which to make his escape. He decided to get his financial accounts in order and to turn them over to the agent who was to bring him the passport. The accounts were muddled, and he had a hard time figuring out the foreign exchange. His first trial balance showed a $2,000 deficit. He did it over again, and the deficit rose sharply. He tried again, but was unable to straighten the accounts out. Then he hit on an idea. He rang for the bell boy and when he appeared, he asked him to bring an abacus. "An abacus?" repeated the bell boy. "Yes, an abacus. Tell the porter, he will give it to you." Some twenty minutes later somebody knocked on the door. A portly middle-aged gentleman, all friendly smiles, extended his plump hand and said in Russian: "Glad to greet a real Russian!" The intelligence agent was taken aback. "The police have tracked me down," flashed through his mind. "When I heard you wanted an abacus, I knew you were Russian ... They don't know here what an abacus means, they use little adding machines. Ah, I remember, our Russian bookkeepers rattled the counters along the brass rods so fast you couldn't see their flying fingers!" After that the effusive man introduced himself. He was the assistant hotel manager, a former major in the Russian Imperial Guards.

All these misadventures were typical of the first unsure steps of the Soviet intelligence officers along the slippery road of the underground. By 1934–35 the Soviet underground intelligence had achieved maturity and grown into a force which no country could ignore.

VI. Entry into the Underground

Even in such a seemingly trivial matter as applying for an entry visa to a foreign country, the underground operative must act with caution and foresight. Before filling out the required questionnaire, he must obtain a copy of the application form and prepare himself to give the right answers. The operative must learn to fill out the questionnaire without any errors in spelling, especially if the language in which he does it is supposed to be his own.

I remember a case when a Soviet operative, masquerading as a Canadian, applied for a visa to India when that country was still in the British Empire. Being deficient in writing English, he struggled with the questionnaire which was laid before him and gave such a horrible performance in English spelling that the British official could not conceal his amazement and called in another official who looked like a typical police sergeant. This man asked the "Canadian" a few questions and eyed him suspiciously. After that he took the passport and disappeared behind a door at the far end of the room. A few minutes later the door opened and the officer came out of a brightly lit closet with the passport in his hand. The operative knew what that meant. The officer who, no doubt, was a security agent had examined the passport under a quartz-mercury-vapor lamp which shows whether there are any fraudulent alterations in the document. Although the visa was granted and the passport did not have any physical defects, the operative canceled his trip because it was clear that he had fallen under suspicion and that he would be put under surveillance during his stay in India.

When entering a country by boat, the traveler is usually required to fill out a debarkation questionnaire and is also orally questioned by an immigration officer. The Soviet intelligence, therefore, instructs its operatives to obtain the questionnaire from the travel bureau in advance and prepare for the talk with the immigration officer. It is only natural that, whenever possible, intelligence operatives try to evade a face-to-face talk with consular or security officials. Thus, instead of applying for an entry visa at a foreign consulate in person, the operative usually stops at one of the best hotels and asks the porter to secure a first-class passage and a visa through a travel agency. This method works out well, but sometimes it produces undesirable complications. Here are examples.

In one instance which came to my attention the false passport given by an operative to the hotel porter for obtaining a visa got lost somewhere between the porter, the travel bureau, and the foreign consulate. Behind such a disappearance there always lingers a suspicion that the security agencies could have had a hand in it. When a bona fide foreign national loses his passport, he can easily get a duplicate after a certain amount of checking and red tape, to be sure. But for an operative who has obtained his passport by fraud, such a procedure is risky. A check by the Passport Division which had issued the passport may turn up unexpected surprises. It may disclose, for instance, that according to the file the applicant had received a passport for foreign travel twice, but that the photographs of the bearer furnished each time were not of the same person. Or it can happen that the two witnesses who had falsely verified under oath the identity of the operative when he had applied for the passport may become frightened when questioned again and, thinking that the fraud has come out, might waver.

One case which caused a great deal of trouble to the NKVD intelligence occurred in 1935. In the summer of that year a top-flight NKVD intelligence officer by the name of Mally was assigned to underground work in the United States. He had a genuine Austrian passport (obtained by fraud in Vienna) and could pass the strictest test as far as the German language was concerned because he had been born and educated in the Austro-Hungarian Empire. However, there was one obstacle which prevented him from going to the United States to take up his new assignment there. The Austrian passports of that period had on them a special stamp which stated that the passport was not valid for travel to the United States.

When Mally applied to the United States consulate in Paris for a visa, he was told there that as long as his passport contained the restrictive clause barring travel to the USA, a visa could not be issued to him. The next step for Mally to take was to go to the Austrian consulate and ask them to insert a correction in the passport making it valid for travel to the United States. However, Mally did not relish the prospect of coming face to face with the consular officials (evidently wishing to avoid probing questions) and, instead, registered at the exclusive Hotel Carlton and asked the head porter to attend to the visa details and book for him a first-class cabin to the United States. But things did not work out the way Mally expected them to. A week or so later, he received a letter from the Austrian consul asking him to drop in at the consulate for a personal talk. But Mally was in a suspicious mood. Instead of dropping in to see the consul, he temporized for about ten days and then told the hotel porter that his trip to America had had to be canceled and asked him to get the passport back. But the consulate told the porter that Mr. Hart (Mally's name in the passport) must come for it in person.

Meanwhile, Mally noticed, or fancied, that he was being shadowed. He checked out of the hotel in a hurry and informed Moscow that he felt he should not go to the consulate to get the passport. Headquarters agreed with him. Having lost touch with its citizen, the Austrian consulate, a few weeks later, informed the authorities in Vienna of his disappearance and mailed the passport back to the Passport Office. A routine investigation that followed revealed that the passport had been issued fraudulently to an unauthorized person by a bribed official. The official was arrested. Fearing that he would confess to issuing other passports as well, the NKVD intelligence sounded an alarm to all its underground rings abroad and ordered a number of operatives with Austrian passports of the same series to leave at once. Thus, a seemingly innocent incident ended in the disruption of the intelligence work on a wide front.

While on the subject of the unpleasant consequences of the loss of a passport, I wish to add that Soviet operatives had instructions to observe the following rule: when crossing by train from one country to another, the operative should remain in his seat, from the moment his passport had been taken from him by the border police for checking, until it has been brought back to him. This advice was prompted by a number of incidents in which Soviet operatives who had absented themselves from their compartments could not be found by the officers who came to return the passports to them. The operatives would soon afterward be confronted by the border police of the next country and, because they were unable at produce their passports, they would be taken off the train and made to wait at a border station for hours until the border police communicated by phone with their counterparts in the neighboring country and arranged that the passports be brought by the next train.

In their travels Soviet operatives often find it necessary to by-pass checkpoints altogether and cross the frontier at points where passports are not required. They also take advantage of buses transporting tourists over a border and back without any formalities, as is usually done between Switzerland, France, Italy, Austria, and between the Scandinavian countries. They also make use of special railway round-trip tickets that allow one to cross from one European country to another for the week end without a passport.

In case of emergency an experienced operative ought to be able to cross the whole of Europe without a passport. Some Soviet operatives are known to have traveled without the benefit of a passport as far as the United States, in spite of the stringent American immigration laws. Some of them came to Canada and Mexico aboard Soviet cargo ships and from there crossed into the United States with somebody's naturalization papers and even settled in the country for long stretches of underground work. Soviet agents are also known to have entered the United States with forged "re-entry cards" which the American immigration authorities ordinarily issue to immigrants in the United States who have not yet become American citizens and need to make a trip abroad.

VII. Business Cover

Besides the false passport the underground operative must have some kind of business cover to justify his permanent residence in the chosen country. The acquisition of a proper and fitting cover is a difficult and important problem in the underground set-up. The operative cannot dodge this problem for the simple reason that a man without an occupation has no proper place in society. "What do you do for a living?" has become an ordinary and legitimate question asked by people everywhere.

Even if the operative possessed a special skill which would ordinarily command a good salaried position, he would not be able to apply for the job because he could not present to his prospective employer data concerning his previous employment. And even if this obstacle could be overcome, the NKVD would not want him to do a full-time job because all his time is needed for his intelligence work.

Experience had shown that the best way to acquire a cover was for the operative to open his own business. During the first years of Moscow's attempts at building the underground organizations, it was fashionable to open something on an attractive scale to make the operative seem prosperous. However, this practice proved costly and far from satisfactory. Here are a few examples:

In the late 1920's the NKVD intelligence supplied one of its operatives by the name of Yury Praslov with a Latvian passport and with a considerable sum of money for the purpose of establishing an export-import firm in France. It was clear from the beginning that the venture was bound to fail. Praslov had no experience as a businessman. His chiefs did not realize that this was not the proper way to create a business. Such enterprises grow from little to big by a natural process of commercial development, if they are able to attract and satisfy the customers and withstand competition. But Praslov's business was created artificially, with beautifully appointed offices and a staff, even before the firm had a single transaction to its credit.

In the meantime, the money provided by Moscow was being rapidly consumed by the payroll and expenses, and the prospects looked very gloomy. Then Praslov, with the permission of his chiefs, turned for help to his friend M. Lomovsky, the head of the Soviet Trade Delegation in Paris. Lomovsky, only too eager to oblige the NKVD, agreed to turn over to Praslov's firm on consignment huge amounts of goods exported by the Soviet Union to France, with the understanding that Praslov would act as a middleman on a commission basis.

The "Latvian" Praslov and his close relations with the Soviet Trade Delegation drew the attention of the French Sûreté Générale, but he was not molested because he was so absorbed in building up his cover that he did not commit a single act of espionage. To impress Moscow, Praslov attracted into his firm a few influential Frenchmen, among them an old titled French lady with an imposing family tree deeply rooted in France's history.

Tens of millions of francs began to flow through Praslov's fingers, and that proved too much for him. Playing the role of a rich man, he was soon swept off his feet by high living. He embezzled about two million francs—about eighty thousand dollars. To retrieve the loss, Praslov took to gambling and became a familiar figure at the Casino de Deauville. Then, one day, I was instructed by Moscow to investigate his firm and books. But that proved unnecessary. In a preliminary talk with Praslov, he admitted to me that he had lost between eight and nine million francs while gambling at Deauville.

Another one in his place would have absconded with the considerable sum of money which he still had in the bank, but he expressed readiness to go back and "be shot." His decision was apparently prompted not only by a sincere sense of guilt, but by the fact that he was married to the sister of Syrtsov, the premier of the Russian Socialist Federated Republic, who was at that time a close henchman of Stalin. About two months prior to all this, Praslov's wife had given birth to a child, and before departing for Leningrad on a Soviet boat he spent two days buying all kinds of things for his baby.

Stalin acted with magnanimity and ordered Praslov deported to the Solovky concentration camp for five years. When his term expired, Praslov decided to stay on at Solovky in a minor administrative position. He said he was ashamed to return to Moscow and face old friends.

Another underground NKVD operative by the name of Tchaikin, a former sailor of the tsarist navy, who had taken an active part in the February Revolution

(1917), came to the United States in 1929 and made an initial investment of a hundred thousand dollars— with bigger sums to follow. With that capital he bought several old merchant ships. At the same time he succeeded in becoming an agent in Hamburg, Germany, for an American automobile company, Graham Paige. The investments kept him busy and little time was left for intelligence work. He gave big parties and was able to report to Moscow that he had entertained admiral so-and-so and congressman so-and-so, but he was unable to impress the home office with his analyses of international relations, which could be picked up in any magazine. The only more or less valuable informant he had was an officer of the American Navy Intelligence.

Tchaikin lived on such a big scale that in Moscow they began to doubt whether he would ever come back to Russia, if recalled. But return he did. In 1931, he made his entry in the Leningrad port in his own ship. He brought with him expensive furniture for twelve rooms and trunks filled with fine things unobtainable in Moscow. He also had a big supply of French wines and liquors and Havana cigars for the chiefs and himself. Tchaikin, who was not an NKVD staff officer and had never worked at the Headquarters, obviously misjudged his chiefs and especially the head of the Foreign Department, M. Trilisser, an ascetic old Bolshevik who had served a term of ten years at hard labor at the dreaded tsarist Katorga. Trilisser was incensed when told that Tchaikin had delivered to his apartment several cases of old vintage wine and liquor and ordered the cases confiscated and sent to a hospital.

For all the money Tchaikin had spent, he could show only a half a dozen doubtful agents and a personal secretary to a top officer in the American Navy. She was a beautiful woman, and Tchaikin lavished plenty of Soviet money on her. Trilisser ordered an investigation into the affairs of Tchaikin, and as a result of it Tchaikin was shot.

Not many underground operatives were as delinquent and derelict of duty as the two I have described. Most of them invested considerable sums of money and, not knowing the business and having little time for it, lost all the money on the upkeep of the staff and on merchandise which was finally sold at a loss.

Wishful thinking on the part of the chiefs of the NKVD intelligence also had an important bearing on the failure of the underground operatives to create and maintain sound business covers. In 1929, the deputy chief of the Foreign Department of OGPU, Sloutsky, conceived a plan according to which an old agent of his would "flee" from the Soviet Union to Germany and, representing himself there as a businessman with anti-Soviet leanings, would open in Berlin a "Bureau for Patents." Sloutsky expected that many German inventors wishing to sell their inventions would flock to the bureau and offer their wares and thus the bureau would be able to select inventions of military value and, where possible, to subvert and bribe known inventors from the German army, navy, and air force.

Sloutsky's choice fell on an agent by the name of Y., whose brother or cousin by the same name served as director of UFA, the well-known German motion picture company. Y. was advanced forty thousand dollars and soon opened luxuriously appointed offices on the Unter den Linden, hired a small staff, and announced in the press through a series of advertisements that the bureau would purchase industrial inventions and was ready to subsidize research by talented inventors.

The response was almost instantaneous. There was a deluge of inventions, mostly concerned with household gadgets, mechanical toys, razors, etc., but no offers containing military or industrial secrets. The only offer of this kind—a new antiaircraft cannon—came from an old professor of mathematics, who happened to be the brother of the chairman of the board of one of the biggest industrial enterprises in Germany. The blueprints and a small model of the cannon were secretly shipped to Moscow. It turned out that the Soviet Commissariat of Defense had already received the same cannon officially from the German General Staff.

Meanwhile, the cost of the cover reached thirty thousand dollars for the first year. The whole construction looked hopeless. The place was full of nonsensical gadgets, but not a single worthwhile invention, or military secret had found its way to the Bureau. Soon the German security agencies became suspicious of the source of the money, and the business had to be liquidated. After such a good life, Y., who was not a member of the party and had no ideological attachment to the Soviet Union, decided that he did not want to return to the drab life of Moscow. He defected amicably without making any revelations and was not bothered by his Soviet employers.

In the early 1930's, the Foreign Department of the NKVD began to ponder seriously a really professional underground network. A brake had been put on indiscriminate spending for foolish business ventures. Candidates for the underground were being selected with greater care, and a few top men of the NKVD intelligence were appointed director-residents to manage the underground work in foreign countries. Each operative was made to study the language of his passport diligently and also the language and history of the country which was to become the base of his operations.

It had also been discovered that an operative could "float" fairly well if he figured as an agent or representative of a business concern from another country. Many such representations were obtained from French, Canadian, Scandinavian, and especially from big American corporations, and the operatives felt more confident having in their pockets imposing business credentials. It had also been discovered that the operatives could set up their own firms with a capital of merely a thousand dollars. Quality stationery and a personal visiting card of the "Director of such and such company" looked to casual acquaintances no less impressive . . .

Some operatives opened little businesses in antiques. Before leaving Moscow, they were given a short course by specialists and supplied, usually through the embassy pouch, with antiques and works of art with a price list and instructions. One of the operatives became a successful dealer in rare first-edition books and manuscripts. Another opened in Paris a news-photo agency which was operated by an expert in that field. Other operatives who were handy with radio equipment or photography opened up photo-studios and radio stores with very little money invested. A few became more or less fictitious correspondents for foreign newspapers.

The most important thing in the arrangement of a business cover is that it should look completely genuine. The operative must remember that he is not in business for the sake of making money, and for that reason he must not overreach himself in commercial dealings and should avoid all lawsuits with competitors or customers. In cases where the operatives figure as agents for foreign concerns, they must try to arrange (usually through the persons who helped them to obtain the agents' credentials) that the concerns regularly mail them price lists, circulars, market analyses, statistical data, and, if possible, similar material from the Chamber of Commerce and the Department of Commerce. Such correspondence with known concerns in his "own" country fortifies the identity of the operative and contributes to his prestige.

Security agencies of all countries know from experience that a respectable occupation of a man may be just a cover for illicit activities, and the physical genuineness of a passport does not always prove conclusively that it belongs by right to the bearer. That is why, when security agencies begin to entertain doubts about the identity of a foreigner in their country, they try to obtain collateral data which might shed light on him. The security officers first look for such evidence in the apartment of the suspect. They secretly obtain entry into his rooms (unlawfully of course, but a practice in every country) and examine his personal belongings, letters, and the contents of the pockets in his wardrobe.

Knowing this, the NKVD intelligence has devised the so-called "secret exhibition" which in a few known cases has proved most effective. This device consists of a series of clues planted by the Soviet agent in his own apartment in such a way that if the clues catch the eye of the secret intruders they will give them proof that the foreigner is indeed the person he represents himself to be. For instance, if the operative lives under a Canadian passport, among his belongings will be scattered a couple of old post cards mailed to his address in Montreal and duly stamped by the post office, a seasonal suburban railway ticket, a public library card from his home town issued in his name, a membership card from a Canadian club, an original telegram delivered to his Montreal address, and a prescription from a Canadian drugstore. The mere sight of a tube of Canadian tooth paste or of accessories used only in Canada or the United States, an invoice from a Canadian department store in the operative's vest pocket, or a crumpled bus ticket will impress the investigators as objective proof. By the same token it must be said that had the secret investigators found in the pockets of the foreign visitor a Moscow bus ticket or a receipt for dues paid to a Soviet trade union, they would be justified in making a different conclusion as to the real identity of the "Canadian."

As a matter of fact, such a case happened in Italy, where the police succeeded in revealing the real identity of a Soviet agent. The Italian detectives searched the agent's apartment in his absence and unearthed a little notebook with Moscow addresses and telephone numbers written in Russian. Had the police known a little more about Moscow, they would have discovered that the notebook read like a who's who in the NKVD.

VIII. Where the Operative Makes His Home

On arrival in the country of his assignment, the operative must turn his attention to the problem of selecting a proper place to live in. The worst place for an operative is a boarding house, for there he is bound to be thrown in contact with people over whose behavior and manners he has no control. During meals in the dining room, they have an opportunity to observe him and to ask personal questions, some of which may be no less pointed than those asked by professional investigators. A boarding house is also bad for another reason. If the operative has attracted the attention of the security agencies they may easily plant a boarder of their own to keep a sharp eye on him.

The best arrangement is to have an apartment in a quiet and conservative neighborhood where tenants rarely say "hello" to each other. Some operatives prefer to live in a good residential hotel, where retired well-to-do people live in an atmosphere of complete privacy. Living there, the operative must avoid using the restaurant or dining room on the premises, because he may unexpectedly come face to face with people who had known him in the past under a different identity. If such a meeting occurs at some other public place, the operative may leave and "get lost." However, if such a chance meeting takes place on the premises of the residential hotel where he lives and where he is registered, the interested persons can easily find out his new name and disguise.

I remember a case which occurred with a friend and former subordinate of mine who worked in the underground in Hitler's Germany and was living as a Canadian citizen in an exclusive residential hotel in Berlin. One evening, he invited a German physician and his wife to dinner at the restaurant of his hotel. Toward the end of the meal he noticed a group of gay people who were having a little banquet a few tables away. Suddenly one of them, a tall slim German with a swastika in his lapel, got up and with a beaming smile made for the table of my friend. Before my friend had time to recognize him, the German was pumping his hand.

"Zdravstvuyte," he shouted in Russian and continued in German. "Glad to see you Herr Ivanov. Do you live here, at this hotel? What suite? I will call you up. We must get together and talk and talk and talk." My friend pretended to be glad to see him and gently led him away from the table.

"Do you work at the embassy here? Are you staying at this hotel? What suite?" asked the German again.

My friend told him that he was in Berlin for a few days only and that he was staying with friends at their villa in Dahlem. "Then call me up," said the German. "Here is my card. Call me up without fail!"

Who was this German? For a year and a half he had been my friend's teacher of the German language at the Berlitz School in Vienna, where my friend served as second secretary of the Soviet embassy.

My friend returned to his table and did his best to play down the incident. He told his guests that the fellow must have had too many drinks and have taken him for somebody else. He said he steered him away from the table fearing that he might decide to sit down with them. My friend's guests did not sense the drama behind the episode and started to relate incidents when they too had been taken for someone else, or when they themselves had mixed up persons who looked remarkably alike. My friend moved out of the hotel and for a time stayed with the family of a reliable German collaborator. When he came to the conclusion that his position had not been compromised, he rented a flat of his own in one of the exclusive suburbs of Berlin.

The cause of the incident, which could have had grave consequences, lay not only in the fact that the Soviet operative, in violation of the existing conspiratorial rules, had used the dining room of the hotel where he lived under a false name. Behind this incident can be seen a bigger and more serious blunder of policy on the part of the NKVD intelligence which allowed officers who had previously served in an official capacity in Soviet embassies and trade delegations abroad to be assigned to underground positions with false papers. There were two main reasons why this was allowed to happen: first, there were not enough qualified officers with the high training, experience, and stamina needed for underground service, and second, the dangerous work in the underground is surrounded in Moscow with such an aura of heroism, that many an intelligence chief, irrespective of his previous service abroad in an official capacity, tries to get the hazardous assignment as a matter of honor and personal pride.

There is an old saying "Tell me who your friends are, and I will tell you who you are." Every underground resident, as well as every operative under him, would do well if he tried to profit by the wisdom of this proverb and acquired respectable and honorable acquaintances. It has been established by the NKVD intelligence that in a number of cases the security agencies of Western countries had temporized and refrained from taking action against a suspected Soviet spy only because the police chiefs were baffled by the respectable and conservative people with whom the suspect associated. Such acquaintances can be picked up at resort places, where people have fun together, at social clubs, educational institutions, and even at church. One NKVD resident, who had been an army chaplain in the past, made a point of regularly entertaining the pastor of the community and his wife, making little contributions to his church, and having an occasional chat with the pastor on the fine points of the Bible. There were instances when an acquaintance would take the Russian agent aside and say: "A man from the Credit Bureau inquired about you. I said you were O.K." In Europe, police detectives often misrepresent themselves as credit bureau researchers. Sometimes such a warning may mean to the intelligence officer the difference between freedom and prison, as can be seen from the following incident:

One underground resident, who was conducting a risky intelligence operation in a certain European country, noticed one day that his personal papers and letters in his apartment had been tampered with. Being of an optimistic turn of mind, he persuaded himself that he was mistaken and that he himself had messed up the papers when he was in a hurry to go out. Then, one evening, when he was having supper at the club with a very conservative bourgeois couple, the wife said to her husband: "Peter, tell him about the detective and what I have told you about it."—"Oh, yes," said the husband, "the other day a man from the

Secret Police, a detective, came to my office and inquired about you. You know, it's their job to snoop around foreigners . . . I told him you were a regular guy."—"And what did *I* tell you about it?" insisted the wife. The husband chuckled and said: "Emma said you must have left behind a jealous girl back home, and she is checking up on you."—"Yes," exclaimed the wife with a giggle. "The first day we met, I told Peter that you must be a Don Juan!" The resident knew that the jig was up. The events of the next few days fully confirmed his apprehensions and he left the country in good time.

When an underground operative runs unexpectedly into a person who had known him in the past under a different identity, he tries to disengage himself from him. But when such an encounter takes place on a speeding train, the retreat is cut off, and he may be in for trouble. It is surprising how many such encounters occurred in the eventful history of the NKVD intelligence. I, personally, have known of at least a half dozen such incidents. Here is one of them:

In the 1930's, the NKVD resident who was directing the underground intelligence in France lived there on a Canadian passport. He left for Rome to supervise an interesting operation which was designed to turn one of the key members of Mussolini's government into a secret Soviet collaborator. When the time for offering a substantial bribe drew near, the resident wrote to the Foreign Department of the NKVD a complete report about the operation and asked for final instructions. While awaiting an answer from Moscow, where the NKVD had to obtain the personal approval of Stalin, the resident decided to go to Capri for a short rest.

He stopped at a middle-class hotel, and when he entered the dining room for his first meal the head waiter conducted him to a small table for two where another guest was already sitting. He turned out to be a young Polish diplomat who had arrived a few days earlier from Vienna where he served as second secretary of the Polish embassy. Soon the two began to take walks together and became constant companions. It is, of course, possible that the Soviet intelligence officer tried to cultivate a little friendship with the Polish diplomat with an eye to his possible recruitment at some later date into the Soviet net.

About a month later, after his return to Paris the Soviet resident was called to Moscow to report on the Italian operation. To avoid having his Canadian passport stamped by the Soviet border police, he went to Moscow on his old Soviet passport. When the Eastern Express reached Berlin and stopped at the Schlesische Banhof station, a few new passengers entered the sleeping car. One of them tapped the Russian on the shoulder and called him by his Canadian name. It was the Pole from Capri. The young man was delighted to see him. He said he was going to Warsaw and expressed hope that his Canadian friend was also going there. The "Canadian" quickly took his bearings and answered that he was going to Tokyo via the Trans-Siberian Railway.

The Pole tried to persuade him to stop in Warsaw and be his guest for a week. He promised to take him to the theaters, to introduce him to beautiful Polish girls, and to arrange a boar hunt at the estate of his father. But the Canadian hardly listened to him. His mind was preoccupied with other thoughts. He knew that in a couple of hours the border police officers would appear, first the German then the Polish, and they would demand passports, and then the Pole would discover that he was not a Canadian but a Soviet national! If that happened the Soviet intelligence officer would not be able to resume underground work in France, where he posed as a representative of a big Canadian concern. His intelligence work in Paris, his passport, and his excellent business cover were at stake.

Some time later, from the far end of the car a sonorous voice announced in German: "Your passports, please!" Our "Canadian" got up quietly and went to the other end of the car and from there to the next car. The Pole waited for him. They intended to go to the dining car together, but the Canadian had suddenly disappeared. He made his way to one of the third-class coaches and waited until the German and Polish police officers had stamped his passport. After that he returned to his sleeping car. The Pole was very much excited. He thought that the Canadian had alighted at the little border station to get some fresh air and had failed to get back on the train.

Such unexpected encounters are the source of constant worry to the underground operative. His mind is automatically attuned to this danger, and whenever he enters a public place, be it a restaurant, theater or hotel lobby he furtively scans the public for a familiar face, always conscious if someone displays an undue interest in him. The Soviet intelligence officer knows that the danger is more real if he has failed to notice that he has been recognized by a hostile person, who may then trail him to his place of residence or business and tip off the authorities. It is thus that some police investigations against Soviet intelligence agents have been initiated.

IX. The Apparatus

When a resident director is assigned to the underground in a foreign country, he may be given the task of taking over an already existing intelligence network or of starting an entirely new one. It is more difficult, of course, to create a new clandestine organization in a hostile country, where all the power of the police and of the counterintelligence agencies is poised against the Soviet intruders who prey on the vital secrets of the nation. But many a resident prefers to build a new apparatus rather than take over an intelligence outfit from somebody else. The reason for this lies in the fact that when an underground resident takes over an existing network he automatically takes over the organic defects lurking in the organization which one fateful day may destroy the network and doom its members to long years of imprisonment. When I speak of defects I have in mind mainly *agent-provocateurs* and counterspies who might have infiltrated the network. Only the experienced resident director who has built everything from scratch can be fairly sure that his apparatus is free from deadly enemies.

The resident director usually has two or more assistants, each of them a staff officer from the Moscow headquarters. The resident and his assistants form the hard core of the organization and, while they must be close-mouthed and on constant guard with almost everyone else, within their own little circle they are able to talk freely and relax. However, in spite of the fact that they are a closely knit band of men, only the resident director and his chief assistant know the whole network and all the operations. The other aides, although staff officers of the KGB, know only those matters which are entrusted to each of them personally. The officers take this with good graces and do not regard it as a manifestation of lack of confidence in them. The justification behind such a policy is the maxim that the less a man knows the less he can tell, and nobody can know the limits of his endurance in case he falls into the hands of the enemy. That such a stringent secretiveness among the members of the *residentura* pays off, was proved a number of times during the last war, when members of the Soviet intelligence rings had fallen into the hands of the Gestapo. The case of Colonel Rudolph Abel also testifies to the soundness of such a policy. As we have seen, Abel's aide, Reino Hayhanen, did not know even where his chief Abel lived and under what name. Neither did he know the other agents and informants with whom Abel was connected. Had he known this, the whole underground organization directed by Abel would have been exposed.

The resident and his aides do not display before outsiders the close association that exists among them. Keeping in mind that if one of them falls under the suspicion of the authorities the others will also be investigated, the relations among them are camouflaged in such a manner as to make them look casual and completely innocent. To be prepared for such an eventuality, the leading partners of the ring work out a legend which traces the origin of their acquaintance and the history of their association, and if they happen to be questioned each of them tells the same story.

The legend is often arranged in such a way as to contain a built in corroboration of their story. For instance, one Soviet resident director used to spend the week ends at a suburban social club where he became well acquainted with the manager of the club. Some time later the assistant of the resident also joined the club. One Saturday night the manager invited a few guests to his suite for supper and a friendly game of cards. At that little party, the manager of the club introduced the assistant resident to the resident director, both of whom pretended that they had not known each other till then.

In some instances the legend of the acquaintance and of the further association is predicated on a legitimate business deal. Thus, for instance, one assistant resident placed an advertisement in the paper offering his numismatic collection for sale. The other assistant resident answered, and the two exchanged letters and the collection changed hands.

Every assistant resident directs his sector of the network which may comprise from 15 per cent to 25 per cent of all the "sources." The assistant resident has under him two to five "group leaders," each maintaining contact with a group of sources. The "group leader" is usually a trustworthy former member of a non-Russian communist party who has been carefully selected and trained for the job. He usually lives on a false passport of his own nationality or of another country in which his native tongue is spoken. If he is German, he may use a German, Austrian, Swiss, or Czechoslovakian passport. If American, he may live on an American, Canadian, British, Australian, or New Zealand passport. If Spanish, he may use the passport of Spain or of any Latin-American country. The "group leader" enjoys the advantages of knowing the language of his passport as a native should. If the "group leader" works secretly in his own country or in a city where his real name is known, he does not assume a false identity and does not use false papers.

The apparatus also has one or two secretaries, usually women, who are in charge of microphotography, typing, and other chores.

The radio operator is the indispensable link between the resident director and Moscow. He is a trustworthy, Moscow-trained technician who knows his trade and is able not only to operate, but to construct a good transmitter if necessary. If the volume of radio communications with Moscow is large, the *residentura* has a code clerk. Otherwise, the job of coding and decoding is done by one of the resident's assistants as a side duty. The *residentura* usually has several transmitters installed at various hideouts, and the transmission is done from various points, sometimes from automobiles in the open country, to make it difficult for the security agencies to track the transmitters down.

"Letter drops," where messages may be left or picked up, and "couriers," who deliver the collected information to an intermediate station or direct to Moscow, complete the basic framework of the intelligence apparatus. If the network is large, the apparatus also has a small passport bureau to fix up passports for unscheduled trips or emergencies and to manufacture border stamps, certificates, and other documents. If the network is small, it uses a passport bureau which services several networks.

The intelligence apparatus directs the work of the so-called "sources"—the men and women who occupy positions of trust in sensitive government organizations of a given foreign state and supply Soviet intelligence with political, diplomatic, military, and industrial secrets of that country. The job of recruiting new "sources" and spreading the net of secret informants wider and deeper into the fiber of the policy-making and other key departments of a foreign government constitutes the most important task of the Soviet intelligence apparatus.

The resident director is the mainspring of the underground organization. He is usually an old hand at intelligence with years of experience as a counterintelligence officer in the Soviet Union. There his job was to ferret out foreign spies who had penetrated the Soviet Union to obtain diplomatic and military secrets. His past experience as a hunter stands him in good stead and proves invaluable when he himself becomes the hunted party in a foreign land. The old NKVD chiefs who had created the Soviet intelligence service looked down with misgivings on the new crop of young officers who had had no previous experience in the field of counterintelligence. They spoke of them condescendingly as of mere messengers who pick up the material from informants for microfilming and bring it back without realizing the complexities of intelligence warfare.

The authority of the resident director is supreme, and in this respect he can be compared to a skipper of a warship or a military commander in the field. He works out the plans of the operations and allocates the tasks among his subordinates. His orders are obeyed promptly, even if the officers do not agree with him. He alone makes the decisions, and the ultimate responsibility is his. He knows that one false step on his part may bring ruin to the network and imprisonment to himself and his men. And although he is under Moscow discipline and must consult headquarters on important operations, he retains a fair degree of independence: Moscow can veto his plan or operation, but it cannot force upon him an operation which he regards as unsound, perilous, or doomed to failure.

Besides his immediate aides, the resident meets personally only the "group leaders" and some of the most valuable and reliable informants. His past in Russia and his new identity (name, passport, business cover and address) are known only to one or two of his closest assistants who are themselves staff officers of the NKVD. Although, for security reasons, the resident cannot afford to become personally acquainted with all the informants and other members of the network, it is important for him to know everyone of them by sight. For that purpose he comes occasionally to meeting places of the "group leaders" with the informants and there takes a good look at each of them from the side lines. The resident must also know the biographical data of each informant, his occupation and place of work, how he has been recruited, his accomplishments for the Soviet intelligence, and the degree of his reliability. The resident holds a key to every informant in the form of a special password with which he can approach him in case of an emergency. Thus, on several occasions when an underground officer of the *residentura* had broken with Moscow, the resident or his assistant immediately approached the informants who had worked with the defector and warned them of the impending danger of exposure and of the countermeasures which must be taken.

I remember a case when the NKVD *residentura* learned that one of its most valuable "sources," a German professor of chemistry, who was conducting important experiments at the Kaiser Wilhelm Institute in Berlin for the German war ministry was on the verge of being arrested by the Gestapo. The Soviet officer who maintained contact with this professor was at that time in a hospital resting after an emergency operation. The professor had to be warned to destroy all traces of his espionage work, dismantle the special photographic equipment which had been installed at his home by a Russian expert, and make his escape. The resident went with one of his employees, a young German woman, to the site of the Kaiser Wilhelm Institute, in Dahlem, and when the professor left the building for home they followed him for some distance to see whether he was being shadowed. When they established that he was not, the woman approached him, identified herself quickly with the password, and broke the bad news to him. She handed him an envelope with money, and the professor was able to carry out the instructions and effect his escape that very night by crossing the border with a false German passport provided for him in a hurry by the *residentura*.

Soviet intelligence officers agree that next to the resident director, who is the daring skipper of the whole intelligence enterprise, the most important figure is the "source," or the informant, as he is usually called. If the informant is situated in a strategic position with access to important diplomatic or military state secrets, he is worth his weight in gold every time he produces something of significance. If the network has only a dozen such informants, the success of the resident director and of the members of his staff is assured, and they are morally amply rewarded for the risks they run. The principal task of the resident and his assistants will then consist in guiding the informants intelligently and in seeing that they are not caught.

Unlike Western intelligence services, Soviet intelligence treats its informants with genuine solicitude. It never violates its promise not to divulge their identity or services in behalf of the Soviet Union, and it rushes to their aid whenever they are in trouble. The Soviet intelligence hires the best lawyers when informants are caught and helps their families with generous sums of money, even when the further usefulness of the informants has been completely destroyed. There have been cases when Soviet intelligence saved informants hours before their impending arrest by getting them out of the country, helped their families with ten-thousand-dollar bank drafts, and later did their best to reunite them with their families by bringing the families to them in the Soviet Union. This solicitude for the informant is based more on considerations of self-interest than on moral or humanitarian grounds. The Soviet intelligence simply came to the conclusion that such a policy toward the informants benefited its cause and contributed to its success.

It is noteworthy that even during Stalin's blood purges in which several dozens of Soviet intelligence chiefs and underground residents perished, the holocaust did not touch the informants, who merely acquired new chiefs after the old ones had been liquidated.

The dangers to which the informant and the officer expose themselves and the joys they share as a result of successful exploits bind them into a bond of genuine friendship, and I have seen many manifestations of sincere devotion and affection on the part of the officers toward the informants. But the irony of it is that the informant rarely knows the real name of his friend, and he has no way of contacting him, once their ways have parted.

X. Recruitment of "Sources"

The recruitment of new informants into the underground network is the most hazardous and difficult task of all intelligence activities. From the very first step the recruiting agent finds himself at a serious disadvantage, because by proposing to a person that he become a spy for the Soviets, the agent exposes his own role even before that person has given his reply. If the answer is negative, the net result remains that the recruiter has *given himself away* . . . This alone shows how skillful and astute the recruiter must be, how softly he must tread to secure a hasty retreat, and what a good judge of men he must be.

Soviet operatives are constantly on the lookout for men and women who are able to deliver important secrets which Russia seeks. The first step is to find out who these people are, where they are, and what they are: their views and beliefs, their private lives and ambitions, their moral character and weaknesses, and above all their potential value as sources of information. People agree to become spies for a number of reasons, such as:

1) Idealistic purposes,
2) Money, career, and other motives of personal gain,
3) Romantic entanglements,
4) Love of adventure,

5) To conceal a committed crime and escape responsibility,

6) Homosexual deviations and other vices.

It will be noticed that I did not mention blackmail as a means of recruitment. Contrary to the general belief, the Soviet intelligence, as a rule, does not employ blackmail in its foreign operations, because it is very dangerous and can boomerang in the face of the recruiting officer. It must be remembered that the Soviet officer operates on the territory of a foreign state and that his fate is in the hands of the informant no less than the fate of the informant is in the hands of the officer. Under such conditions it is too dangerous to make an enemy of a man and thereafter rely on him in such a delicate and hazardous matter as an intelligence operation. There were actual cases when blackmailed persons turned for help to the authorities, made a clean breast of their transgressions, and won forgiveness for themselves by helping the security agencies trap the Soviet recruiting agent.

The reason why it is generally believed that Soviet intelligence agents in various countries employ blackmail to press people into the service of Soviet espionage is that when spies working for Russia are occasionally caught they try to extenuate their guilt in the eyes of the jury and to win as much leniency as they can from the court by saying that they have been forced into espionage by Russian threats and blackmail.

There were, of course, rare exceptions when blackmail seemed to be the right shortcut to acquiring a valuable informant, but experience has taught the chiefs of Soviet intelligence that, in the conditions of intelligence operations abroad, the best way to assure the effective co-operation and devotion of the informants is to be straightforward with them at all times. Therein lies one of the secrets of the spectacular successes of Soviet intelligence.

From the point of view of human motivation, a rich variety of reasons, calculations, and emotions guide people into the perilous undertakings of espionage. The skillful builder of a network who selects and lures people into the adventures of intelligence and guides them in the endless battle of wits bears considerable similarity to the creative novelist, with one major difference—the novelist traces on paper the emotions and actions of imaginary characters. The builder of the spy net inspires and directs the feelings and actions of real people. If the author of fiction makes his characters act irrationally and contrary to their own psychological make-up, the literary critic will immediately spot and denounce the deadly sin of unbelievability, whereas if the creator of the intelligence scheme allows himself to introduce illogical and unbelievable combinations, his plans will fall through and his live characters will soon find themselves behind bars. That is why the ability of the operative to conceive a sound intelligence scheme involving a group of people with diverse interests and to make them co-operate in providing vital information to the Soviet Union is considered a high mark of intelligence competence.

In their operative work the Soviet intelligence officers prefer to deal with men and women who are devoted to the ideals of communism or are in sympathy with the aims and policies of the Soviet Union, because such people give all they have and may be relied on. Some outstanding successes of Soviet intelligence have been attained through the dedicated service of informants of this category, and in those cases when some of them were caught, they took the full measure of punishment without trying to win leniency by giving their confederates away. However, the Soviet government frowns on the use of card-carrying members of foreign communist parties for espionage activities, because this gives the enemies of communism the chance to assert that communist parties in every country are mere adjuncts of the espionage agencies of the Soviet Union, rather than bona fide political parties.

The next numerous category of informants consists of people who work for money. This is a clear-cut arrangement. The Soviet Union is ready to pay well, and it encourages such informants with bonuses and gifts for outstanding achievements. To this group have belonged noted foreign diplomats, including a few ambassadors, and a number of high-ranking general staff officers. Soviet intelligence keeps, however, a wary eye on informants of this category lest they offer their wares simultaneously to another country as well. Such an act on the part of an informant is considered treacherous, and he is quickly brought into line by a stiff warning. Sometimes an informant who works for money loses his nerve and decides to discontinue working for the Soviets. In such a case, no duress is applied to him. The intelligence officer assumes the role of a solicitous friend. He tries to bolster up the morale of the informant and offers him a two- or three-month furlough with full pay, and when that period expires, the officer presents to him a new plan of work in which the risks are reduced to a minimum. For example, the number of meetings might be brought down to one a month, and the informant is no longer required to steal secret documents, but to bring oral information instead.

Collaboration based on romantic interests is not relished by Soviet intelligence officers not only because it is morally disgusting, but also because it is bothersome in the extreme, usually short-lived, as most love affairs are, and sometimes ends up in an explosion which ruins the whole intelligence scheme. The few officers who did practice that method were looked down on by their colleagues and were referred to contemptuously as the "matchmakers."

The "romantic" method was evolved as a result of the constant efforts by the Soviet intelligence to enroll into its service young women who work as secretaries, stenographers, code clerks, and administrative assistants in important departments of foreign governments, such as departments of defense or foreign offices, especially those women who work as private secretaries to members of the Cabinet.

The routine is the same as practiced by intelligence services of other countries. Young women dream of love and marriage. The Soviet intelligence is ready to provide the first and to hold out a promise of the second. Carefully selected young men, with good looks, manners, and education, seek acquaintance first with friends and relatives of the girls and later are introduced through them to the girls themselves.

When the sponsored romance blossoms into a love affair, which is sometimes accompanied by a formal or secret engagement, a suitable piece of confidence game is devised in order to explain to the girl why her Romeo wishes to read the secret documents which pass through her hands. He may tell her, for instance, that he has been offered the post of diplomatic correspondent for a foreign newspaper, a position which will at last secure him financially and allow them to get married. But to make good on his new job, he may add, he would have to see from time to time the diplomatic dispatches ... In those cases where the intellectual level and social background of the girl justify it, the young lover may use a more direct approach and open to her the lofty ideals of socialism and justice for the exploited masses, and, if the girl is impressed and interested, he gradually brings her to the realization that they must help the Soviet Union with information about the anti-Soviet intrigues of the wily capitalists.

In 1930 an attractive young secretary at the German Ministry of Foreign Affairs, who took pride in her Nordic type of beauty and was in sympathy with the Nazis, began to pilfer secret diplomatic dispatches for her lover whom she believed to be an ardent follower of Hitler, but who in reality was a German communist in the employ of the Soviet intelligence.

Amazing as it may seem, some of the deceitful love affairs sponsored by the NKVD intelligence ended in true and lasting marriages. I have personally known two such cases. Every time such a thing happened, the chief of the Foreign Department of the NKVD, Artouzov, would chuckle and say: "This couple will have an interesting story to tell to their grandchildren when asked how they happened to get married."

Love is by no means the only method by which secretaries have been enticed into the intelligence net. Some of the girls have been recruited by other means as well—such as money—often with the help of close relatives.

I remember an interesting case that took place in Germany in the early 1930's. At that time there lived in Berlin a middle-aged German gentleman, Mr. C, who had been brought up and educated in Russia, where he owned a large pencil factory. The pencils with his name imprinted in gold were known to every school child in Russia. When the Russian Revolution had taken place, Mr. C lost all his holdings and fled to Germany with his family. By 1931 he lived with his wife and their exceedingly charming young daughter in quite strained financial circumstances.

One day a Soviet intelligence officer came to see Mr. C with an interesting proposition. Having introduced himself as a member of the Board of the Soviet Commissariat for Light Industry, the officer told him that in spite of all the efforts made in Russia they were unable to produce a satisfactory pencil, and the Soviet Commissariat would like Mr. C to go to Russia and to organize the production of pencils on a national scale. The officer said that C would be given a large salary in German marks and in Russian rubles, a liberal expense account, and a permanent visa for travel to Russia and back. The Russian asked him to work out a plan for the construction of a number of such factories in various parts of Russia and to make his recommendations concerning the purchase of machinery in Germany. Mr. C was overwhelmed. An impoverished millionaire, he had come to the sad realization that he was an aging gentleman whom nobody wanted or needed, and suddenly—such a fantastic offer!

The Russian told Mr C that he was going back to

Russia where the project would be discussed at the highest level and that he would visit Berlin again in a month. He gave him a few thousand marks and asked him to start working on the project. A month later the officer reappeared and told C that the project had been examined in Moscow and that an approval by the government was assured. However, he warned him of one serious snag. The Russian NKVD had information that C was closely connected with the Japanese embassy in Berlin and for that reason it was considered dangerous to entrust a big project to a man who might be a secret agent of the Japanese intelligence service. "Was this true?" asked the officer. C was taken aback and hastened to refute the accusation. He insisted that he had nothing to do with the Japanese, except having been invited once or twice to a diplomatic reception as an act of courtesy toward his daughter who happened to be the personal secretary to the Japanese chargé d'affaires and at times to the ambassador himself. His daughter, he said, was completely nonpolitical and had been employed by the embassy only because of her knowledge of foreign languages and the excellent references that were given her by important people.

The fact that C's daughter worked for the embassy was, of course, no news to the Soviet officer. It was exactly because the NKVD intelligence had known that she was confidential secretary to the Japanese chargé d'affaires that the intelligence officer was sent to her father with the lucrative business proposition. At that time the work of the NKVD intelligence in Japan was very poor, and the prospect of obtaining a valuable source of information in the Japanese embassy in Berlin looked very tempting, indeed. The officer then told C that he knew of only one way to placate the NKVD, and that was for the daughter to agree to keep the Soviets posted about the diplomatic moves of the Japanese government in Germany and especially about the policy of Japan toward the Soviet Union. The officer promised C that no one would ever learn about this. After some hesitation C agreed to ask his daughter to bring him copies of the Japanese diplomatic dispatches and the coded cables that passed through her hands. He said that he and his daughter were tremendously devoted to each other, and that there was nothing in the world she would not do for him. Of course, he added, this would have to be kept secret from his wife. And, as if to brush away his moral scruples, C declared that the Japs meant nothing to him anyway, whereas Russia was his second motherland where he had felt himself a Russian. He confided to the officer that the chargé d'affaires, a highly educated man and perfect gentleman, was desperately in love with his daughter, but that, of course, he would never agree to having little Japs for grandchildren.

In the meantime, C was putting his final touches to the project. He enjoyed being entertained in exclusive restaurants and insisted on playing host to the Russian. Both men were in high spirits. Each felt that he was near the realization of his goal.

A day or two later, they met for dinner. C appeared suddenly changed. He looked crestfallen. "I have ruined everything!" he said. "My tongue did it." And then he explained. He said that on the preceding night, when he and his wife were in their beds hopefully talking about the unexpected good luck, his tongue let out the secret about the Russian request. "That did it!" he said. "She jumped out of bed as if obsessed and shouted hysterically, 'Over my dead body! My darling daughter will never be a spy!' You know women," he added apologetically.

Although the plan of the NKVD did not succeed, I relate this story to illustrate how painstakingly a recruiting operation is prepared and what methods are sometimes employed.

Every informant who works in a strategic department of a foreign government is asked by the Soviet intelligence officer to furnish information about the service records and personal lives of the personnel. This information is studied by the intelligence officer with a view to possible recruitment of some of the employees into the Soviet net. A secretary of one department may happen to be friendly or very close to another secretary of the same or a different department. However, as a rule, Soviet intelligence will not use one secretary for the recruitment of another, because this would expose the connection of the first secretary with the Russian intelligence, while there is no assurance that the second secretary would agree to collaborate. A third person is usually assigned to do the direct recruiting, while the informant may be asked to stay closer to her girl friend and try to learn how she reacts to the recruitment and whether there is a danger that she might denounce the recruiting agent to the authorities. The following story will illustrate how this is done.

A Soviet underground resident in Paris was informed by a "source" of his, a girl who worked as a filing clerk at the French Foreign Ministry, that her girl friend, a secretary of the same department, had been asked by the Deputy Foreign Minister to be his private secretary. Moscow became very interested, and the resident was given instructions to spare no efforts to enroll her in the intelligence net. Here is how the resident started out to do this. He instructed the filing clerk (his informant) to invite the newly promoted secretary to the Comédie-Française for the opening night of a new play. Two seats next to the girls were occupied by two dashing young Englishmen who spoke fluent French. During the most humorous moments of the performance which evoked much laughter in the audience, one of the young men, who pretended to know less French than he actually did, turned to the girls for enlightenment. The girls, especially the one privy to the plot, tried to oblige *l'étranger*, whose witty quips made the girls laugh the more. During the intermission they chatted together. One of the young men introduced himself as a writer, which he was not, and the other as a pianist, which he really was, and a good one to boot.

At the conclusion of the performance the young men asked the girls to an exclusive night spot for supper. Although the private secretary raised her brows superciliously, ready to refuse, the other expressed consent from both of them.

This artificially contrived acquaintance gradually began to yield results. After a few more meetings of the four together, the "writer" began to date the private secretary tête-à-tête. A few weeks later she confided to her girl friend that she was in love. When the "writer" left Paris to return home to Wales, she became unhappy. She wrote to him and he answered with long distance calls, sometimes from another city, and with flowers. Then he suddenly fell silent. Her letters to him remained unanswered. The girl lost peace of mind. She had to see her girl friend every day just to talk about him. She could not sleep. This was love . . .

A month or two later, the "writer" reappeared in Paris. He said he had broken with his despot father, a rich landlord, who wanted him to marry the daughter of an old friend, another landlord. When he broke his engagement to the girl (till then he had never mentioned he was engaged), his enraged father disowned him and cut off his allowance. He still had money in the bank to last him for a year, but he was determined to manage his own life. He would never stoop to ask the cruel old man for help! Further, he told the girl that he had been commissioned by a British publisher to write an important book on the state of Europe. He was determined to make the book a success. His whole career now depended on this!

The "writer" rented a flat in the Latin Quarter of Paris and there surrounded himself with stacks of books and papers on the history and diplomacy of Europe. Every day he made extensive notes, typed excerpts, and was "hard at work" till his belle arrived from work to have dinner and spend the evening with him. Soon they were secretly engaged at a party which comprised the original foursome that had first met at the Comédie-Française. He told her they would get married after the book had reached the booksellers' stands. Although he was supposed to stretch his savings carefully to last for a year, he could not refrain from spending money on little gifts for her and entertainment, and she chided him for that. Well, what was to be expected from a spoiled son of a rich man who never had to work for a living!

Then the inevitable came. One day he broached to her that he was confident his book could be a resounding success if only she would help him with the documentary sources from the place of her work, mainly with the ambassadorial reports to the Quai d'Orsay. The girl was not shocked. It was so natural that she should help him and she was happy to do it. She only wanted to be sure that the publisher would know nothing about it, and that the book would not contain verbatim quotations from the diplomatic documents or any reference to them. This he could promise her in good conscience.

Some of the most valuable and devoted informants in the Soviet net were foreign civil servants and military men, with access to state secrets who, by force of circumstances, had committed a crime and faced imminent discovery, but were saved by the Soviet intelligence from disgrace and imprisonment in the nick of time.

One such case took place in France: a Soviet underground resident was tipped off by a reliable informant in the French Ministry of War that a friend of his, a major of the General Staff, had gambled away government money and was desperately looking for a way out. A Soviet operative immediately got in touch with the desperate man and covered the deficit. This major became one of the most valuable "sources" and was so grateful that for a long time he declined to accept a regular monthly salary that was offered him.

Another case occurred in Berlin. One night, in 1936, the door bell rang at the suburban villa of Gordon, the Soviet resident director in Berlin. Gordon, who was already in bed, came to the door. There stood a respectable-looking gentleman who said he wanted to talk to him. When Gordon hesitated, the stranger said: "Maybe, if I call you Rudolph, you will feel that this may be important to you. "Rudolph" was Gordon's secret code name. From the subdued tremor in his voice Gordon could see that the man was under severe strain. He let him in. As soon as the visitor introduced himself, Gordon knew who he was. He was assistant chief of the Russian section of Hitler's military intelligence. This man had embezzled a large sum of money. An audit of the secret funds had been ordered, and if he was found out he would be court-martialed. He needed help. He volunteered to open to Gordon "all his cards." Rudolph asked the visitor whether he could give proof of good faith. The German anticipated this question. He took out of his breast pocket several photostats of secret reports written to Moscow by the Soviet military attaché in Berlin. He gave the name of the Soviet officer in the Commissariat of Defense in Moscow, a Russianized German from the Volga region, who had stolen these secret documents for the German military attaché in Moscow.

Gordon immediately called up the Soviet military attaché and asked him to come to the embassy. There Gordon showed him the photostats. The attaché confirmed that he had written them, the last one only a month before.

The sum required was too large for Gordon to take full responsibility on himself, but if the German were to be saved, they had to act fast. There was no time to waste on coding cables to Moscow and waiting for a reply. The same night, Gordon called up an unlisted private line in the home of Agranov, deputy commissar of the NKVD, and in Aesopian language hinted at the situation to him. The payment was sanctioned.

During Hitler's times the NKVD intelligence in Germany acted very cautiously not only because it was afraid of the Gestapo, but also because it feared Stalin,

who in case of a spy scandal in Germany would be-
rate the NKVD for jeopardizing his relations with
Hitler. For that reason, Soviet operatives would strive,
when possible, to have meetings with important German informants not in Germany proper, but in a neighboring country such as Denmark or Czechoslovakia.

However, with the newly acquired German informant, resident Gordon found a more convenient way of
maintaining contact. Taking advantage of the fact that
the informant was assistant chief of the Russian section
of the German military intelligence, he brought him together with a Russian girl-clerk from the Soviet consulate and advised the German to pretend that he had
enrolled the girl in the German military intelligence as
an informer on the personnel of the Soviet embassy.
The German welcomed the idea. And thus the girl
would bring to the rendezvous a typewritten report on
some trivial matter concerning the consulate and receive from the German little rolls of film with information that really counted.

As we have seen, the two major tasks of the NKVD
intelligence consist of recruiting informants among the
government employees of foreign countries and using
them for the purpose of stealing state secrets of foreign
nations for the benefit of the Soviet Union. The higher
a secret informant is placed in the government department, the more valuable he usually is. That is why the
NKVD intelligence officers strive constantly, where
possible, to help their informants obtain promotions
in their government service. The Soviet officers do this
by dispensing good advice to the informants, by covering their expenses for social entertainment of colleagues
in the service to build up goodwill, and, on rare occa-

sions, by using the influence of a trusted informant who happens to occupy an executive position in the department concerned. If the resident director carries influence with headquarters, he does this at his own discretion, but ordinarily the sanction of Moscow is required for such an operation in which the name of one informant has to be disclosed to another.

However, in spite of all the efforts expended by Soviet intelligence officers to help their informants attain promotions in government service, the results were spotty and far from satisfactory. Only in the early 1930's did one of the chiefs of the NKVD intelligence hit upon an idea which solved this most difficult problem as if by magic. He succeeded because he approached the problem not only as an intelligence man, but as a sociologist as well. This officer took account of the fact that in capitalistic countries lucrative appointments and quick promotion are usually assured to young men who belong to the upper class, especially to sons of political leaders, high government officials, influential members of parliament, etc. To them promotion is almost automatic, and it does not surprise anyone if a young man of this background, fresh from college, passes the civil service examinations with the greatest of ease and is suddenly appointed private secretary to a cabinet member and in a few short years assistant to a member of the government.

Accordingly, in the early 1930's, the NKVD *residenturas* concentrated their energy on recruitment of young men of influential families. The political climate of that period was very favorable for such an undertaking, and the young generation was receptive to libertarian theories and to the sublime ideas of making the world safe from the menace of Fascism and of abolishing the exploitation of man by man. This was the main theme on which NKVD *residenturas* based their appeal to young men who were tired of a tedious life in the stifling atmosphere of their privileged class. And when the young men reached the stage when their thinking made them ripe for joining the Communist party, they were told that they could be much more useful to the movement if they stayed away from the party, concealed their political views, and entered the "revolutionary underground." The idea of joining a "secret society" held a strong appeal for the young people who dreamed of a better world and of heroic deeds.

A very important part in influencing the young men was played by idealistic young women of various nationalities who already had a smattering of Marxian theory and who acted as a powerful stimulus which spurred the young converts to action. Having been brought up first by governesses as sissies and later sent to exclusive private schools, they were charmed by the daring Amazons, and their intellectual association with them often blossomed into romances which frequently culminated in marriages. These young men hardly regarded themselves as spies or intelligence agents. They did not want anything for themselves—least of all money. What they wanted was a purpose in life, and it seemed to them that they had found it. By their mental make-up and outlook they remind one very much of the young Russian Decembrists of the past century, and they brought into the Soviet intelligence the true fervor of new converts and the idealism which their intelligence chiefs had lost long ago.

The NKVD intelligence no longer worried about attaining promotions for their charges. The promotions came automatically, and the NKVD chiefs looked forward with great anticipation to seeing some of the new recruits in ambassadorial posts a few years hence.

XI. Clandestine Meetings. Eluding Surveillance

In the life of an underground operative nothing is as simple as it is in the lives of ordinary, carefree people. Even such a trivial matter as making an appointment with another person must be planned with care, arranged with absolute clarity that precludes any possibility of misunderstanding, and carried out with the maximum of safety. When naming a place for the meeting, both parties must make sure that they have in mind the same place, that such a place really exists, and that it will be accessible at the time of the proposed meeting. It is surprising how many meetings went astray because the above-mentioned details had not been taken into account. I remember an incident when the deputy chief of the Foreign Department of the NKVD, Loginov, arranged by wire to meet the Soviet underground resident in France, Kepp. Both agreed to come to Vienna on a certain day and put up at the Park Hotel. Both duly arrived on the date, but could not find each other. On the third day of waiting Kepp, who was under strict orders to stay away from Soviet embassies, went to the Soviet embassy to find out where Loginov was. There he learned from the local resident that Loginov had left a few hours before for Moscow, furious at Kepp for not having kept the appointment. Kepp was baffled. He swore that he stopped at the Park Hotel and produced the key to his room. On that key was written: "Park

Hotel Schoenbrun," which was famous and well known. But Loginov stopped at another, little known, "Park Hotel."

A similar incident occurred in New York, where two underground officers of the Red Army intelligence, by the name of Stern and Gorev, were supposed to stop at the St. George Hotel. One of them stopped at the St. George Hotel in Brooklyn and the other at the hotel by the same name in Manhattan.

Another resident was instructed by cable from Moscow to meet an agent in Paris at the well-known restaurant Duval on Rue Madeleine, in the center of the city. This was a place at which the resident used to dine often when he had served in Paris a few years before. To his surprise he could not find the restaurant. Puzzled, he turned for information to a policeman on duty not far away. The policeman explained that the restaurant had been closed for over a year and the place rebuilt by a piano-producing firm for its showrooms. "Amazing!" chuckled the policeman. "You are the second tourist who within five minutes asked me about the Duval restaurant. There he is!" said the policeman and pointed to a man who was reading a theatrical announcement on the wall, a dozen steps away.

Another intelligence officer, who a few years before had worked in Germany, by wire instructed a secret agent to meet him at a certain hour inside a well-known bank on the Friedrichstrasse in Berlin. This appointment was faulty on two accounts: first, the meeting was set for a day when all the banks were closed, and, second, as it turned out, the massive building of the bank had vanished from the face of the earth, having been demolished and replaced by a modern office building.

Experience has taught intelligence officers to arrange appointments with more care and foresight and to set two or three consecutive appointments at different places and hours to make sure that if one meeting does not come off, the other will.

Often, meetings are arranged between people who have never seen each other before, and steps must be taken to insure that they recognize and identify each other without fail. In such cases it is especially important that both parties should appear at the predetermined place promptly on time. Both persons must be supplied, first, with general recognition data of each other. For instance, A must be told that B, whom he is going to meet, is forty years old, five feet, ten inches tall, stout, with dark hair, and wears hornrimmed glasses. Then the specific details follow: B will wear a blue coat, gray felt hat, and a polka dot tie. He will have a certain magazine in his hand.

The procedure may then demand that A should approach B and start a prearranged dialogue, which may run like this: "Say, haven't we met recently at Al Grosby's party?"—"Oh, yes, of course we have, but that was not at Grosby's. It was at Madame Gates's cocktail party."

Sometimes, the procedure of recognition requires that each party produce a previously stipulated object which cannot be easily duplicated. For instance, A and B produce each a dollar bill, both bills bearing consecutive numbers. There was a time when intelligence services of a number of countries used to divide a unique object in two parts and give one part to each of the meeting parties. However, the NKVD intelligence discontinued this practice after the Polish counterintelligence service arrested two Soviet secret agents each of whom had a half of the same dollar bill in his wallet. Thus, from a means of identification, the two halves of the paper dollar became proof that the two Russians, who denied knowing each other, belonged to the same conspiratorial organization.

The prearranged dialogue between both parties, which serves as a kind of password, must be specific, otherwise it may be misleading and cause trouble, as can be seen from the following incident. A young Soviet operative in Germany was sent to a certain suburban bus stop in Berlin and instructed to meet there a courier unknown to him and hand over to him a little box of talcum, inside of which there was a roll of secret films. At the bus stop the young man immediately spotted the person who fully answered the description of the man he was supposed to meet. He approached the man, smiled at him and said: "I am here as a tourist, I admire your beautiful country."—"Yes, it is beautiful. I am also a tourist," answered the man. His answer was letter perfect. The young operative, who related the story to me, said he was about to hand over the package to the stranger, when the latter suddenly said: "That's my bus!" and quickly boarded the vehicle.

Meetings may be regular or special. The regular ones take place—usually between the same contact and "source"—at certain intervals in accordance with a prearranged routine schedule. If for some reason one party fails to appear, the meeting is expected to take place the next day at the same time, if no other variations have been agreed to. The officer and the "source" must have an understanding that if, for some unforeseen reason, contact between them has been lost, both of them must come on a certain day, or days, to a certain place. This is known as a "control meeting."

There, the one who has failed to keep the previous appointments must give a sign as to whether he can be approached, and if he can the meeting takes place.

The intelligence officer must always be conscious of the fact that his telephone and those of his confederates may be tapped. Therefore, he must not use his own telephone for communications with any one of the members of the *residentura* proper or of the network. The best thing is to use public telephones for such occasions. When the officer makes an appointment with an informant over the telephone, he must try to throw the eavesdroppers off the track by juggling the time and place of the meeting. For instance, if he wants to see the informant on Wednesday at 8 P.M., he tells him that he would like to meet him on Thursday at 9 P.M. If he adds "at your place" or "at my place," it may mean Café de Paris or restaurant Petit Chat, respectively. In case the officer has serious reason to suspect that the telephone of the person he is calling might be tapped, he must be doubly cautious. When the informant answers, the officer may pretend that he dialed the wrong number, excuse himself in a specified form, and hang up. This will serve as a signal to the informant that he should come to a certain public telephone where the officer will call him up in one hour, and, if the informant cannot make it, then in another half an hour. Both parties must agree in advance on the meaning of a few indispensable phrases and terms which would allow them to convey to each other the simplest things of their trade. Concise coded expressions must be invented for emergency situations which would enable the informant to tell his superiors that he is being shadowed, that his apartment has been searched by the police, that the officers have seized compromising data, and so on. Diverting a call from a private to a public phone is widely practiced by Soviet intelligence agents because this offers the possibility of talking freely without fear of the wire being tapped. In this way an officer may keep in touch with several informants daily, using a number of public telephones. However, in this procedure there is one disadvantage that should not be lost sight of. If the informant happens to be a traitor or a plant, then the police may tape the whole conversation, a thing they would not be able to do so easily if the officer had a face to face conversation with the informant.

It is absolutely incumbent upon the intelligence officer and the informant to establish whether they are being shadowed and to make sure that they have come to their rendezvous completely "clean" and that neither of them has brought to the meeting place a "tail" behind himself. If one of them, on the way to the meeting, notices or feels that he is being shadowed, he has no right to keep the appointment. In case surveillance has been discovered at the very place of the meeting, or immediately thereafter, it is important to find out which of the two participants had originally fallen under the suspicion of the investigative agencies. If it can be established, for instance, that it was A who attracted the attention of the secret police, he can go back in his analysis of the recent past and try to find the rotten link or contact that pointed the finger at him.

Every intelligence officer must periodically check himself against possible surveillance. This can best be done at leisure by taking long walks or rides to secluded places, where the traffic is very light and where it is easy to see whether one is being "tailed." This kind of checking is not designed to shake off the trackers, but to make sure whether or not there is surveillance. However, it is quite a different matter when the officer sets out to keep an appointment, especially when secret documents are going to be passed. Here the officer must not only make sure that he is not being trailed, but he is required to use every ruse known to him to shake off any real or imaginary trackers whom he might have failed to notice.

The officer may take a passing taxi and follow a route on which it should not be difficult to determine whether another car is trailing him. The fact that a car, which to the discomfiture of the officer has been dog-gedly following his taxi, has suddenly turned off the road and disappeared, does not mean that the taxi is no longer being trailed. Another car may suddenly appear behind the taxi, and this one may belong to a string of police cars that follow one another at a discreet distance, too far to be seen clearly by the officer in the taxi. To mislead and lull the officer further this car may also turn off the road, only to be replaced by still another vehicle. When a well-managed secret police is bent on trailing a serious "customer," it tries to foresee every eventuality and prepares foot surveillants as well as a brigade of motorcars which maintain contact by radio and pass the suspect to each other's care in the same way as football players pass a ball to one another. If the officer is satisfied with the results of the taxi ride, he may then resort to the so-called "filter" method. He enters a department store, or a big hotel, lingers not far from the elevators and jumps into the elevator seconds before it goes up. If nobody enters the elevator after him, he can be sure that no surveillant has caught up with him. Then he leaves the elevator on one of the upper floors, crosses to another elevator, or to the escalator (or the stairway), comes down, and goes out by a different exit. A few minutes later he hails a passing taxi and goes to his destination. There are many other ways to avoid trackers, and, if the officer has not become lax and negligent, he may feel confident that he will not bring surveillants to the meeting place.

As a rule the operative must check himself carefully again after the meeting, especially if he is going to keep another appointment. This precaution is needed for two reasons: Although the operative may feel confident that he has arrived at the meeting place "clean," he can never be completely sure that the other party has succeeded in doing the same; and one must always keep in mind that the other party may turn out to be a double who has infiltrated the Soviet network, or a person who started out as a bona fide informant, but under the influence of some unknown circumstances has changed sides in midstream.

Because the safety of the intelligence officer depends a great deal on whether his informants are able to come to the appointments without bringing a "tail" behind them, it is important that the intelligence officer should teach his informants how they should check themselves against surveillance and what methods they should employ to shake off real or supposed surveillants. It is even more important to see to it that the "group leaders," whose job it is to meet informants regularly, should never let down their guard against enemy surveillance. For that purpose, it is recommended that the *residentura* should, once in a while, trail each "group leader" when he is on his way to keep an appointment (without his knowledge) and thus test his alertness and skill in discovering and dodging trackers.

If there is even a slight suspicion that the informant may have been planted by the police, it is sometimes useful for the intelligence officer to put his meeting with that man under observation. As an example, I may refer to a case which actually happened in Paris. A Soviet intelligence officer had an appointment at a big cafe with a high official of the French Ministry of Commerce who had hinted to the Soviet trade representative in France that he would like to co-operate with the Russians and who had actually turned over to him classified data concerning the trade policy of the French government toward Russia. Setting out to keep the appointment with the Frenchman, whom he intended to enlist in the network, the intelligence officer dispatched to the cafe two of his agents with instructions to watch his rendezvous with the Frenchman from the side lines. During the meeting the Russian officer noticed that two men sitting a few tables away were stealthily but sharply observing him. "Those two men look like police agents," remarked the Russian to the French official.—"Oh, no," retorted the Frenchman. "To me they look like typical middlemen, brokers, I should say, who conduct their business from cafes."

When the interview was over, the Russian was the first to leave the cafe. A few minutes later, the Frenchman went over to the table of the two men and the three of them engaged in an animated talk. One of the Russian observers, who sat not far from their table, was able to make out that they were talking about "le canaille russe" and the Comintern. Then they ordered a meal. The check was picked up by one of the original occupants of the table. The three men left together in the same taxi. Thus, the crude attempt of the French police to plant a "double" was nipped in the bud.

Clandestine meetings may be held in a great variety of places: private apartments, hotels, restaurants, automobiles, offices, libraries, museums, physicians' or dentists' offices, etc. The choice of place depends on many imponderables and often on whether the parties intend to have a long discussion, or a short talk, or a "silent meeting." The so-called silent meetings are designed to eliminate the obviousness of the communication between the two participants and to deceive the surveillants. Such meetings are usually held in parks, museums, libraries, and similar places. For instance, the operative and the "source" pretend to be studying some reference material at the library. Both, independently of each other, make notes while sitting or standing side by side, or opposite each other; then one of the two departs and, instead of taking his own notebook, or folder, picks up that of his neighbor. Or, while perusing a number of books, one of them slips an envelope into a certain volume, which his neighbor retrieves a little later. Only an experienced detective, who knows who the two "researchers" are, could detect such a sleight-of-hand trick. There are other variations of the same technique: Two persons separately enter a movie theater and take adjacent seats. There, under the cover of darkness, one passes the material to the other. Or the two find themselves together on the same bench in the park. One of them has brought a magazine or newspaper which he puts on the bench between himself and the other person. When nobody is around to notice, the other picks up the magazine (with the envelope inside it) and walks away.

In important cases the NKVD intelligence relies heavily on trusted dentists and physicians who help to cover up clandestine meetings. The dentist, for instance, reserves a convenient hour (usually at the end of the reception time) for two of his clients who pass through the dentist's office into a back room. Later, they leave separately by a side door.

I remember a curious incident that occurred in Berlin, where a Soviet underground operative and his "source" were conferring in the reception room of a dentist's office. Although the dentist had no more appointments, the doorbell rang. With the secretary gone for the day, the dentist had to answer the door himself. But before doing that, he put one of his "clients" in the dental chair and the other in the back room, behind the office. Then he admitted a middle-aged man who complained of a sudden toothache. The dentist asked him to wait and returned to his patient. When the two men left the office by a side door, the dentist put the new client in the chair. He saw at once that the patient was feigning pain. He told the man that there was nothing wrong with his teeth, ascribed the pain to a temporary state of neuralgia, and did not charge him anything for the examination.

The client was obviously impressed with the professional competence and honesty of the dentist. "I see that you are an honest man," he said, "and I am sure that you are a good German as well." After that compliment he produced his identity card of a police detective and asked the dentist for information about his previous patient. The detective had in mind the

Soviet operative. He confided to the dentist that the Gestapo had information that the man was a Comintern agent. He asked the dentist to try to find out, in the course of a friendly chat, where the suspected Russian had been born, where his wife was, and what her first name was. The detective volunteered information that she was a graduate of the Lenin School in Moscow. He did not evince interest in the other man.

The warning was God sent. The next day the operative was out of the country. The "source" was put in quarantine for a couple of months, and when the resident was satisfied that the man was not under police observation contact with him was resumed.

Western counterintelligence and security agencies, as a rule, rarely employ women for outdoor trailing of suspected spies. This self-imposed limitation, was successfully used by the NKVD intelligence to counteract surveillants, and in a few cases literally stopped the trackers in their tracks. Often, when important documents had to be passed from the "source" to the operative or back, the *residentura* employed two women as couriers. The women would enter a restaurant or cafeteria separately and sit at different tables. Then, a few minutes apart, they would go to the ladies' room, where one of them would transmit the documents to the other, sometimes in a silent operation by each picking up the other's handbags. The eager detectives would thus find themselves suddenly barred, when their quarry disappeared behind the forbidden door.

As I have already mentioned, the "source" or informant is the most important figure in the Soviet intelligence set-up because without him no secret information of any value could be obtained. The principal function of the staff of the *residentura* is to direct the work of each informant, to teach him how to do his work effectively, and to guard him against mistakes that may prove fatal.

The staff officer of the *residentura* is obliged to know the personal history of the informant, the circumstances under which he was recruited, the quality of the work which he was able to render, his personal traits and character, and the extent of his reliability. In order to be able to judge the actual and potential possibilities of the informant, the officer must study all the details concerning the official position which the informant occupies in the government department, the nature of his work, the names and positions of his immediate superiors, his relations with the other members of the staff, the extent of his authority, and whether he has legal access to the secret documents or manages to get hold of them unlawfully. The officer must know how classified materials circulate through the department, how many persons within the department have access to various categories of secret documents, and whether the informant has, or may obtain, access to the safe, keys, and combinations.

No detail should be overlooked by the officer, no matter how insignificant, because it is often the small detail that traps the informant. I remember an incident when an experienced officer taught a young recruit at length how he should take out a certain document of great importance from the safe of the German war ministry. When, a few days later, the young man came to the rendezvous with the officer, beaming with pride, the officer was shocked to see the young man take the precious document out of his breast pocket. It was on a half a dozen pages of legal size and had been folded neatly in four to fit the pocket. This was not the informant's fault. The responsibility lay with the officer who failed to warn the new recruit that a stolen document should never be folded because this proves conclusively that the paper has been taken out and carried in a pocket. Such a slip can alert the security agencies and prompt them to institute surveillance inside and outside the department and resort to a number of devices, such as electric-eye photography or coating the secret files with invisible finger-printing substances, to entrap the intruder.

The officer must become the counselor and tutor of the informant and guide him not only in his spy work but in his official career as well, striving to attain promotions for him, and, when it is in the interests of Soviet intelligence, to get him transferred to another section or department, where his usefulness to the Soviets can be greater. Often such a transfer is sought by the Soviet intelligence when the department in which the informant is employed is well covered by other secret informants, whereas another department or section still waits to be infiltrated.

To take secret documents from a file is a delicate and risky affair, and the officer must explain to the informant that he does not want him to take out papers indiscriminately just because they happen to be stamped "secret" or "top secret." As a rule, the informant is advised to report first what kind of documents he has seen, and only after that is he told which of the papers to bring, if any. Only when the informant is highly developed politically and has had long experience in intelligence work is he permitted to exercise his own judgment and snatch important papers, while the snatching is good.

Mature and serious intelligence officers do not subject their informants to unnecessary risks and are satisfied to receive oral reports about the content of classified papers. They instruct the informant to steal secret documents only when they contain important information, or when an opportunity presents itself to photostat documentary evidence that a foreign state or group of states is hatching, behind the scenes, a conspiracy against the Soviet Union. In one case the Russian Politburo attached so much importance to certain foreign documents that it was not satisfied with the photostats obtained by the NKVD intelligence and demanded that one of the original documents be stolen, which was duly accomplished.

Some ambitious careerists among the Soviet intelligence officers prod their informants to steal documents marked "top secret," with high-sounding letterheads such as "Office of the Foreign Minister" or "Committee of Imperial Defense," with the sole purpose of impressing Moscow with their ability to rummage freely in the secret files of a foreign government. How dull some of such stolen documents are can be seen from the famous "pumpkin" papers obtained by the Soviet secret agent Whittaker Chambers from the American State Department, papers which contained neither state secrets nor information of any value or interest to the Soviet Union.

When instructing the informant in the matter of lifting secret documents, the officer must take into account many technical details, such as the minimum time required for the operation, whether the papers might be missed, where they should be photographed, and how they should be restored to the files. To save time, some of the informants are taught to photograph documents.

In such cases the informants must be furnished not with specialized photographic equipment, but with the kind of camera that any amateur photographer might have. Only in cases in which the informant has to deal with large scientific and technological blueprints is he supplied with specialized equipment, which is usually installed for him by Russian experts. Skilled in filming documents, the informant may take the classified papers on the way to lunch and bring them back into the office immediately after lunch. To justify his claim to being an amateur photographer, the informant is advised to have at his home family pictures and other innocent snapshots lying around.

XII. Bait

The activity of the intelligence service is aggressive and *offensive*. Its agents go out boldly to steal and rob the vital secrets of a foreign nation. The activity of the counterintelligence is *defensive*. Its duty is to protect the state secrets of the nation, to uncover foreign spies, and to render them harmless. Both forces are engaged in an endless battle of wits. We hear more often of fabulous feats carried out by spies against all odds— diplomatic papers stolen, atomic secrets carried away, blueprints of atomic submarines transmitted to a foreign power, secret code experts fleeing to Russia. And almost always we hear that the barn was locked after the horse was stolen. The work of the intelligence agent is dangerous, the work of the counterintelligence agent is safe but very difficult.

A Soviet intelligence agent in a foreign country may come to grief in a number of ways: a government employee whom he lures into the Soviet network may denounce him to the security police, or a Foreign Office clerk who has been observed stealing classified documents may be trailed to the meeting place with the Soviet agent, or photographs of stolen papers may accidentally be left in a taxi, or the true identity of the Soviet agent may suddenly come to light as a result of an unhappy encounter... Such blows come suddenly from unexpected quarters, and there is not much the agent can do. However, there are critical moments in the life of the underground agent when he knows that he may be walking into a trap, but, being carried away by excessive zeal and the instinct of a gambler, he challenges fate itself and loses.

These moments usually occur when the counterintelligence agency of the government (or the secret police) succeeds in planting attractive *bait* in the path of the Soviet operative and dangles it on and off so temptingly that the latter succumbs to wishful thinking and swallows it. Then he is hooked for good. I have seen experienced intelligence chiefs, who had never failed to warn their subordinates against the fallacy of wishful thinking, themselves succumb to it.

The first symptom of bait is that it is planted so conveniently that is too good to be true. One of the ways to distinguish bait from a bona fide opportunity is to examine closely how the opportunity has presented itself and whether the Soviet agent, or somebody's unseen hand, was holding the initiative. The distinguishing line between a "plant" and the real thing is so thin that sometimes a bona fide offer is rejected for fear of a trap. One of the most valuable informants the NKVD ever had, a lieutenant-colonel of the German General Staff, was first turned down when he offered his services to the military attaché of the Soviet embassy in Berlin.

A year later, an NKVD underground resident in Berlin, contrary to the warnings of his superiors, approached the same colonel and came to terms with him. The resident told him frankly that he did not trust him, but was willing to try him out. He offered him a substantial monthly salary and a bonus for every paper adjudged valuable and arranged that the colonel should photograph the documents himself and bring the rolls of film to Prague or Copenhagen. The first delivery contained such important and completely authentic documents that it became clear that there was no hoax or "plant" involved. One of the papers containing data on the annual production of German bomber planes had already been received previously from another, absolutely reliable, source. When a few months later the colonel expressed apprehension that his frequent trips abroad might arouse suspicion, the resident again defied the advice of his superiors and began to accept the films from the German in Berlin, in the office of a trusted physician. Had the resident been searched by the Gestapo after his emergence from the physician's office, they would have found nothing. The rolls of films were always carried out of the office (without the knowledge of the colonel) by another "patient."

The fear of falling into a trap set through planted informants is so deep seated in the minds of undercover Soviet intelligence officers that there were cases when the NKVD intelligence dropped valuable informants from its net on the basis of inconclusive suspicion. The following will illustrate the point.

One day a well-dressed man entered the Soviet embassy in Czechoslovakia. He told the Russian receptionist that he wished to see someone of the top personnel of the embassy on a very important matter. He declined to give his name to the receptionist. After some hesitation, the Soviet vice-consul, an NKVD man, agreed to talk to him. The visitor came straight to the point. He said he was an official of the Foreign Office of a European country (which he named), that he got himself into financial difficulties and decided to offer his services to the U.S.S.R. He produced a few samples of what he could deliver—carbon copies of diplomatic exchanges between the Foreign Office of his country with its ambassador in Moscow. Although the vice-consul, with an air of offended innocence, remarked that the Soviet embassy did not engage in that kind of underhanded activities, the visitor left the papers and a telephone number with the consul and explained how he could be summoned to a meeting.

The carbon copies were dispatched to the Home Office for analysis and were found to be authentic. After that, Moscow instructed one of its underground residents in Europe to check up on that man and, if no adverse information turned up, approach him with the utmost caution because he might be a "plant." As a result, contact was established and the *residentura* began to receive copies of diplomatic correspondence from the new informant, not only with that country's embassy in Moscow, but also with its embassies in Poland, Romania, Bulgaria, and other Eastern European states. The new source began to grow in importance after the so-called "Little Council," which evaluated all incoming intelligence data for the Politburo, became interested in the circular letters on the international situation sent by the Foreign Office to its ambassadors abroad for orientation.

In the meantime, Moscow continued to confirm the authenticity of the material received from the new source. Then suddenly things began to happen. One day, the Home Office wired to the underground resident that it had obtained (through another *residentura*) a photostat of the payroll of the Foreign Office and that the name of the newly acquired "source" was not on it. Moscow ordered meetings with the man discontinued until further notice and that he be taken under close surveillance. Moscow expressed apprehension that the man was a "plant" and that the secret police were feeding the *residentura* with authentic material in order to uncover as many members of the Soviet ring as possible. The surveillance soon disclosed that every morning the new informant went to a government agency which dealt with affairs of war veterans and was apparently working there. Informed about this, Moscow ordered a break with the man for good, and the officer who had maintained contact with him was recalled to Russia for fear of his arrest.

The contact man, an intelligent and brave young officer who was proud of his first successful assignment, felt that he was being robbed of a great opportunity. He did not share the apprehensions of the chiefs and begged to be allowed, before leaving the country, to have a last talk with the man and find out what had made him behave in the way he did. In this he had the support of the resident director, his immediate chief. By the time Moscow acceded to his entreaties, he had skipped two or three appointments with the informant. Fearing that the young officer might be seized if the secret police had advance notice of the forthcoming appointment, the resident instructed the officer to wait for the man near the War Veterans Building at the end of the working day, to follow him for some distance in order to make sure that he was alone, and then to accost him and invite him for a talk. Two other Soviet operatives were instructed to trail the officer just in case and to watch the developments.

The man was caught off base when the young officer suddenly confronted him and asked for an explanation. Startled and confused, he admitted that he had never worked at the Foreign Office and that he was an official of the veterans' administration. Why did he misrepresent himself? His explanation sounded plausible. He said that he was shielding another person from whom he was getting the carbon copies. It was his widowed sister, employed as a confidential secretary and chief stenographer in the East-European Department of the Foreign Office. The Russian demanded proof. None was immediately available. Then the officer proposed the following acid test: the man should immediately call up his sister and ask her to join him at a certain cafe. There he should introduce him to her and say: "This is the gentleman who receives the carbon copies from me. He knows now everything. Please, do not be afraid and answer all his questions truthfully." The man agreed to the test. But soon serious doubts began to creep into the mind of the Soviet officer. The informant was calling up his sister every fifteen minutes for two hours, but nobody answered the telephone. Was he calling up the right number? Was he making a mockery of him? Suddenly the telephone was answered. The sister had just returned home. She was told to take a taxi and come right away, which she did. The woman was shocked by the strange confrontation with a foreigner and answered his questions in a quivering voice. But everything proved to be on the level. She showed her identity card from the Foreign Office and was even able to enumerate some of the papers which she had thus far transmitted to her brother. The persistence of the young officer paid, and it saved the NKVD intelligence a valuable source of information.

When the security police plant false informants, they have in mind the following aims:

To get in contact first with one Soviet intelligence agent and then, by putting him under close surveillance, to find out the identity of other Soviet agents and the people they meet;

At a critical juncture in international relations mislead the Soviet policymakers with false and provocative information;

And, finally, to seize at least one Soviet intelligence agent with *stolen government papers in his possession,* arrest all of his known and suspected accomplices, and, after a thorough investigation, put them on trial.

To convict a man in a civilized country on a charge of espionage, substantial proof is needed, proof which can meet the requirements of the *law of evidence.* It is not enough for the police or the examining magistrate to be convinced that the suspect is a spy. The mere fact that a person has a false passport may be punishable according to law, but to convict him of espionage more weighty proof is needed. That is why police and other security agencies strive so hard to seize the suspect with the "goods"—with the material proof of espionage activity *in his possession.*

Soviet intelligence officers know this and are constantly reminded by Headquarters of the necessity of taking stringent measures to avoid being caught with incriminating documents. When a false informant has been successfully planted by the secret police, the police detectives know in advance when and where their man will meet the Soviet agent to turn over to him the "stolen" classified papers and the exact place and time when he will get these papers back from the agent. Knowing this, the police can easily seize the Soviet agent with the incriminating documents in his possession. This danger is always on the minds of the Soviet intelligence officers, but no matter what the risk, they have to receive the secret papers from the informant and later return them to him. How to do it with the maximum of safety is the responsibility of the underground resident.

Every resident tries to solve this dilemma in his own way. But before discussing the ways and means of evading a trap, I shall introduce a few cases which illustrate how the police and counterintelligence agencies use a "plant" in order to catch the intelligence officer. One of the most notorious cases was that of a Russianized Pole Kazimir Baransky, an NKVD intelligence man, who served as second secretary of the Soviet embassy in Warsaw under the name of Kazimir Kobetsky. In 1923, when the Soviet government was deliberating a plan to send troops through Poland to Germany, Baransky received an order to blow up the stores of dynamite and munitions in the Warsaw fortress. Baransky carried out that dangerous assignment on October 12, 1923.

The Poles learned that the explosion in the Warsaw fortress had been engineered by their fellow Pole, Kazimir Kobetsky. But they did not demand his recall and decided to catch him in some other act and then take a full measure of revenge. Such an occasion presented itself only a year later. The Polish counterintelligence service managed with considerable ingenuity to plant an *agent provocateur* in Baransky's service—a clerk in the Polish Foreign Office. To whet Baransky's appetite the man began to supply the Soviet embassy with authentic documents from the Foreign Office. Gradually, the *agent provocateur* insinuated himself into Baransky's confidence, and Baransky began to meet him personally. One day in the summer of 1925, Kazimir Baransky was to meet the agent in order to return to him several documents from the Polish Foreign Office, among which there was a very interesting report from the Polish ambassador in Japan, Patek. Finally, the Polish counterintelligence managed to lure its enemy into a trap.

When Baransky arrived at the meeting place, he noticed suspicious characters displaying a marked interest in him. Baransky tried to slip away, but the police detectives began to close in. He made a dash out of the encirclement, thinking only of how to get rid of the compromising documents in his pocket. Darting into a side street, he entered the Church of St. Catherine. There he knelt, shoved the papers into a pew, and left the church by another exit to Jerusalem Street. At that moment the agents, who had lost him, caught sight of him. They seized Baransky and subjected him to a thorough search. When they didn't find the expected documents, they became enraged and beat him. They trampled him with their boots and inflicted severe blows on his head and face. Baransky lost consciousness, and when he came to he found himself in police headquarters. Some time later, the diplomatic papers and Ambassador Patek's report from Tokyo were found in the church. This case created a furor. Angry diplomatic notes were exchanged between Moscow and Warsaw, and Baransky was recalled. Had he been an underground resident without the protection of a Soviet diplomatic passport, he would have been at the mercy of his enemies, and the Soviet government would have disclaimed any knowledge of him.

Before analyzing this case from the point of view of intelligence technique, I shall introduce another one that took place in Moscow a few years ago. The KGB (Soviet Committee of State Security) succeeded in planting a false informant who insinuated himself into the confidence of the assistant military attaché of a leading Western country. One day, while riding in a crowded bus, the informant and the attaché silently exchanged packages. The attaché received from the informant a notebook and in turn gave him a package of what looked like a neat bundle of Soviet money. Someone in the bus raised a hue and cry and demanded to know what was in the packages. An obviously stage-managed commotion started, and the bus stopped. A band of police agents were, of course, on hand, waiting. They entered the bus—a mere block from his embassy—grabbed the attaché, dragged him out, roughed him up, threw him into a waiting car, and brought him into one of the police offices. There, alternating threats of physical violence and offers of large sums of money, they demanded that the attaché change sides and become a spy for the Soviets. The notebook received from the informant, they insisted, contained espionage information written in invisible ink. This was probably so, because the Soviet KGB had planted the notebook in the first place. The attaché was shaken by the violent ordeal, but did not yield. As a result, he was expelled from the Soviet Union. Had this man not been an official of a foreign embassy, but an underground agent, he would have disappeared and never been heard of again.

These two simple cases illustrate how the "plant" scheme works and how the trap is sprung. Now we can examine them more closely and see what mistakes were committed that led the intelligence officers to their debacles. In each case there were two major underlying faults:

Wishful thinking on the part of both intelligence

officers which made them trust planted counterspies, and;

failure of each officer to take proper measures to insure himself against being caught with incriminating material. And it must be underlined here that *there are effective means to thwart the actions of police detectives,* even when they are being helped by planted informers.

When intelligence officer Baransky was being chased by the Polish detectives, the one pulsating thought in his mind was how to get rid of the incriminating documents in his breast pocket. It is true that he had succeeded in outrunning his pursuers and jettisoning the ambassador's report and the other papers. But he could have been overtaken before he darted into the church. Baransky's belated wish not to have had the classified documents on himself could have been fulfilled had he foreseen the possibility of a trap and prepared for it.

What could he have done? How could he go to the meeting without taking the documents with him when the sole purpose of the meeting was to return the papers to the informant? Yes, Baransky could and should have gone there without the documents. Before setting out to keep the appointment, he ought to have given the documents to an aide with instructions to wait for him at a certain place, for instance in a suburban restaurant, three to five miles away. Then he could go to the meeting place. If the informant did not appear and Baransky were seized and searched, the police detectives would have found nothing on him and would have been completely frustrated. The very fact of the search would have given sufficient proof that the informant was a "plant," and the police would have lost a valuable counterspy whom they had groomed and planted with such difficulty.

If the informant did come to the meeting and Baransky noticed that the place was surrounded by aggressive-looking detectives, he could tell the informant that he was unable to bring the documents and then part with him for good without ever returning the papers. If the meeting place seemed clear of detectives, Baransky could hail a taxi and take a pleasure ride with the informant along a quiet route—to see whether they were being trailed—and only then drive to the restaurant where the aide was waiting. There, Baransky could absent himself for a few minutes, pick up the documents, rejoin the informant, and return them to him.

In the case of the assistant attaché dragged out of the bus in Moscow, there were still bigger mistakes committed, and the manhandled official has to blame himself and those who had trained him for intelligence work for his misfortune. To pick a crowded bus for the transmittal of secret data and money is a blunder which defies all logic. The bus was utilized by the KGB (Committee of State Security) as a veritable mousetrap which afforded its detectives the possibility to observe the exchange of packages at close range, and at the same time the attaché was deprived of the possibility of changing his mind, retreating, or escaping. It is a pity that a man who had the stamina to withstand the initial shock and the brutal police coercion that followed did not get proper training in his own country.

There are two distinct moments when the secret police may spring the trap on the Soviet intelligence officer who has fallen for the bait. The first is, when the Russian meets the false informant to *take* the classified government data from him. The second moment is when the Russian comes back later to *return* the photographed documents to the "informant." Which of the two moments is the more dangerous?

Experience has shown that in countries where counterintelligence is ably conducted, the secret police prefer to seize and search the Soviet agent not when he receives the classified papers from the "informant," but when he comes to *return* them to him. Following these tactics, the police gain two advantages: (1) they can be 99 per cent sure that the Russian, who comes with the sole purpose of returning the documents, will have them in his possession when searched, and (2) the police can instruct the "informant" not to appear for the appointment and thus conceal his unsavory role in the whole affair. On the other hand, if the police try to apprehend the Russian at the moment he is receiving the documents from the "informant," the detectives— who must keep at a distance in order not to frighten the Russian away—may misinterpret a gesture or movement made by one or both men and swoop on the Russian and search him prematurely, only to find that he has not yet taken possession of the incriminating documents. There is also the danger, from the point of view of the police, that the Russian, having received the documents, may suddenly jump into a passing taxi or dart into the subway and slip away. Chasing him may end in failure, and after that the Russian would not walk into the same trap again.

In the case of the Soviet intelligence officer Baransky, I indicated how he could have thwarted the police detectives who searched him when he came to *return* the diplomatic papers to the false informant.

But a Soviet intelligence officer can also thwart the attempt of the police to seize him when he comes to *receive* the documents from the informant. This can be done in the following way: Even if the Soviet officer has complete confidence in the informant, he should never take the documents from him at the place where they have met. Instead, the officer should hail a passing taxi and together with the informant ride out of any possible encirclement, real or fancied, and only then, when he is completely sure that he is free from surveillance, should he take the incriminating documents.

In this connection we may recall the celebrated case of the Soviet intelligence officer Valentine Gubichev (formally an official of the U.N.) and Judy Coplon, employee of the U.S. Justice Department. When Gubichev had his last and fateful meeting with Miss Coplon in New York, he refrained from taking the secret reports which she had stolen for the Soviet because he was not sure whether both of them had come to the meeting place without being trailed by security agents. To find this out, he took a long walk with Miss Coplon, then they rode in subway trains and changed to a bus, but Gubichev still hesitated and did not touch the incriminating reports for fear that they might be shadowed. Finally, when the government agents apprehended and searched both of them, the report was found not in Gubichev's possession but in Miss Coplon's handbag, a circumstance which had an important bearing on the case. Gubichev apparently remembered his lessons from the intelligence school. He knew that he was obliged to check himself against possible surveillance and not to take the incriminating material unless he felt sure that he was not being shadowed. But his mistake lay in the fact that when he met Judy Coplon and sensed that something was wrong, he did not take effective measures to shake off the surveillants. What he did was to ride endlessly with her in subway trains and buses, as if their trackers could not do the same thing.

The best remedy against bait-swallowing is common sense, suppression of wishful thinking, critical analysis of all available facts, and a sound appraisal of all the people involved. One more ingredient, which is possessed only by very few intelligence men, is intuition of a kind which is almost uncanny. Such men, who possess it, are usually called in for consultation in serious cases, when a final decision has to be taken.

But no matter how clever the intelligence officer is, he may some day meet his match in the person of a crafty and imaginative counterintelligence agent who will skillfully plant irresistible bait in his path and beat him at his own game. A counterintelligence agent of that caliber can devise and camouflage a trap with such ingenuity that even the most experienced eye will not detect the treacherous props and the fine threads leading to it. At no time will this counterintelligence agent push his adversary in the direction of the bait or introduce into the plot elements which may reveal somebody's sinister initiative behind it. On the contrary, the intended victim will be made to feel that nobody lures him anywhere and that he acts according to his free will and choice. The following case that took place in France years ago may serve as an example.

A young NKVD officer who worked in the underground in Paris, where he posed as a Czechoslovakian national, enrolled in a course of anthropology at the Sorbonne for the purpose of improving his French. There he became acquainted with a French student, also studying anthropology. Both men were enthusiastic billiard players and often, after classes, they went out to play for an hour or two. In this way the Russian was able to converse in French. The French student was poor, and the Russian was glad to pay for the billiards and the drinks and would from time to time lend his friend a hundred francs. They never talked politics, but the Russian noticed that his friend was buying the socialist paper *Populaire*. One day the French student told the Russian that he would have to discontinue his studies for lack of money and look for a steady job to support himself and his ailing mother. In a somewhat embarrassed way he promised that some day he would repay to the Russian (whom he thought to be Czechoslovakian) the eight or so hundred francs he owed him. The Russian was touched and made him accept another five hundred francs "until better times." After that, the Frenchman discontinued coming to the lectures.

Then one Sunday, three months later, while strolling along the Avenue de l'Opéra the Russian caught sight of his French friend briskly crossing the broad avenue ahead of him. The Russian increased his pace and caught up with him on the other side of the avenue. Both were glad to see each other. The young Frenchman told his friend that with the help of his fiancée's father he got a job as a photographer at the Second Bureau of the General Staff of the Army and that, although he was photostating a lot of supposedly important papers and maps, the salary was too small for him to venture into marriage and at the same time take care of his mother. His only hope, he said, was to find a better paying job. He wanted the Russian to meet his fiancée and gave him his telephone number. Both agreed to see each other soon.

The NKVD officer was struck by the unexpected opportunity which had suddenly knocked on his door. He knew that the NKVD intelligence had long been coveting the secrets locked up in the Second Bureau (military intelligence) of the French General Staff and hurried to the resident director to report the good news.

Both men discussed and analyzed the details of the officer's acquaintance and relations with the Frenchman. Here was a young man who badly needed a steady income sufficient to enable him to get married and take care of his ailing mother. The Russian officer was on a very friendly footing with him, and the *residentura* had the money necessary to bail his friend out of financial difficulties and help him get married and settled in comparative comfort. The fact that the young Frenchman was reading the socialist *Populaire* was also a welcome sign, because as a socialist he could hardly be an enemy of the Soviet Union and, moreover, a Russian Marxist and French socialist could always be counted on to find a common ground.

The perennial fear of a trap did not bother the resident and his officer. Nowhere could they find in the relations between the Soviet officer and the Frenchman a discordant note which would indicate that the friendship had been artificially contrived and nurtured. There was no trace of a possible "plant," because the young Frenchman had never asked him a tactless or prying personal question and had never said or done anything which could be intended as a decoy to inveigle the Russian into a trap. In their relations the initiative was always on the side of the Russian. It was the Russian who first accosted the young man and talked to him—as he did to many at the Sorbonne. It was he who each time invited the French student to a game of billiards and to have a drink. Had the Russian not caught sight of the young man when the latter was crossing Avenue de l'Opera, their relations might have never been resumed. And again, it was not the Frenchman who stopped the Russian in the street, but the other way around.

The two intelligence officers discarded completely the possibility of a "plant." They decided to go ahead and devised a way in which the offer should be presented to the Frenchman. But before taking the final step, the resident advised the officer to accelerate his friendship with the young man still further, to meet his fiancée, and to try to learn the occupation and social position of her father, who was able to produce for his daughter's boy friend a job at the Deuxième Bureau. Meanwhile, a parallel check had been ordered and it disclosed that the father of the fiancée was an old army sergeant working in the war ministry as an office manager, with influence far beyond his low rank. The Russian officer met the girl of his friend and helped him finance the purchase of an engagement ring. Finally, it was decided that the time was ripe for the recruiting job, and the resident wrote a perfunctory report to Headquarters and was waiting for the green light to complete the operation.

In the meantime, an old Soviet informant who was an officer of the French Sûreté Générale (Secret Police) and who had been dropped by the Soviet "legal" *residentura* a year earlier for insubordination and other sins, got in touch with his former Soviet contact. This informant was an agent of the Sûreté Générale in charge of narcotic violations, but had proved able in the past, soon after the sensational kidnapping by Soviet agents of the former tsarist General Koutiepov in Paris, to steal the whole file of the Sûreté on that kidnapping and bring it to the Soviet agents for photostating. He apparently missed the additional salary which he used to get from the Russians and wanted to be reinstated in their secret service. He brought with him an interesting memorandum which he had stolen from his place of work which showed that the Sûreté Générale had received information from one of its informants within the French Communist party that a certain Czechoslovakian by the name of X., who was residing in Paris and attending the Sorbonne, was in reality a Soviet national and agent of the Soviet intelligence service. It transpired from the memorandum further that the Sûreté had dispatched a young agent to the Sorbonne with instructions to enroll there as a student and get acquainted with the suspected Soviet agent.

This brilliant piece of counterintelligence work was thus revealed in the nick of time. The "legal" resident transmitted the information to Moscow, and the NKVD Headquarters immediately wired back to the underground resident an order to desist from the recruiting operation. The Soviet intelligence officer was ordered to leave and the group of his informants was "put on ice."

The resident and the intended victim of the trap could not but admire the subtle workmanship of the French inspector and the dissimulating skill of his young agent. Both Soviet officers noticed how cleverly the encounter on the Avenue de l'Opéra was stage managed to make it look completely accidental, once more leaving the initiative to the Russian.

I have described this episode in some detail to show with what consummate skill bait can be planted and how deadly a small team of two counterintelligence men can be.

XIII. Communications

The secret information gathered by the underground *residenturas* in foreign countries would be next to useless if it could not be channeled speedily to Moscow and, duly processed, presented to the policy-making organs of the Soviet government. The maintenance of efficient communications between the intelligence apparatus in Moscow and its underground ramifications all over the world is, therefore, of paramount importance. During the first years, when the underground rings abroad were being created, the problem of communications was an easy one. At that time the underground *residenturas* were serviced by the diplomatic couriers of the Soviet Commissariat of Foreign Affairs, via the Soviet embassies. The Foreign Department of the NKVD used to send its mail to the underground rings in foreign countries by addressing it in care of the "legal" resident at the Soviet embassy. The legal resident would then notify the underground resident and transmit to him the mail through a reliable contact. The underground resident, in his turn, would use the same channel to dispatch his mail to headquarters in Moscow, via the Soviet embassy and the diplomatic pouch.

From the point of view of safety and speed, this method of communication was the easiest and the most effective. However, it had its limitations. The underground *residenturas* were organized to function not only in peace time, but in war time as well, and if they depended exclusively on the embassy's diplomatic pouch for communication with Moscow, they would find themselves cut off completely, the moment the diplomatic relations between the country where the *residentura* is located and the Soviet Union had been broken off. Even in peace time, the connection of the underground with the diplomatic courier service is considered undesirable, because it contradicts the basic premise on which the creation of underground intelligence has been predicated. The principal reason why the underground *residenturas* were created at all was that the Soviet government wanted to be able to disclaim all responsibility for the espionage activity of its agents in case they were caught.

As a result of a number of adjustments and reorganizations, there exist today four channels of communications between the KGB intelligence and its *residenturas* abroad:

The Diplomatic Courier Line which connects the Home Office, in Moscow, with its legal *residenturas* abroad, based in Soviet embassies.

The Direct Underground Line, through which communications flow from the Home Office in Moscow direct to underground *residenturas* in a number of countries and back.

The Indirect Underground Line, along which communications flow between Moscow and the underground through an *Intermediate Underground Mail Station* in a country adjacent to the one in which the recipient *residentura* is situated. For instance, the mail from Moscow to the underground *residentura* in Rome is taken first to an underground mail station in Lausanne, Switzerland, and from there to its final destination in Rome.

The Mixed Line, through which the mail proceeds from Moscow *by diplomatic pouch* to the Soviet embassy in a foreign country, and from there *by underground courier* to the underground *residentura* in an adjacent country. For example, the mail assigned to the underground *residentura* in Berlin goes by the diplomatic pouch to the Soviet embassy in Copenhagen. From there it is taken by an underground courier to the underground *residentura* in Berlin.

The intermediate underground mail stations are set up preferably in small countries—Switzerland, Holland, or Denmark—which have been regarded for many decades as territories not likely to be drawn into a war between great powers. The intermediate stations stand a better chance to function undisturbed in traditionally neutral countries, which explains why a country like Switzerland is a hotbed of espionage activity and international intrigue in every big war. The intermediate underground mail station has no intelligence operations of its own and acts only as a "letter drop" and a courier service for short distances. It serves underground *residenturas* in one or more adjacent countries where the real espionage work is being done. It is manned mostly by one or more native citizens of the neutral country, often a man and wife ideologically devoted to the Soviet Union but not known as communists. They have especially contrived hiding places for the mail they transmit, but they do not know what is in it. They do not even see the little slides or rolls of film concealed in a binding of a book, toilet accessory, or in any other innocent-looking object. Now microfilms can be hidden in hollowed out tiny objects like cufflinks, jewelry, coins, etc. In time of war the mail station may harbor also a radio man and a transmitter.

As a rule, the operators of the mail station do not know the underground residents or the members of their staffs personally. If they have something to transmit, they notify the *residentura* by calling up a certain telephone number, or sending a telegram or picture post card to a certain address. The character of the picture may denote a special message. A sea view may mean one thing, mountains—something else, and various kinds of animals or flowers—many other things. Usually, the *residentura* sends a courier to the town where the mail station is situated to pick up the messages from Moscow or to deliver its mail for the Home Office. But sometimes, the mail station delivers the mail to the *residentura* by courier.

One of the most difficult tasks in securing the underground lines of communications is to select couriers who can justify their frequent trips to various countries and who are at the same time completely reliable. In view of such requirements, the Soviet intelligence has to acquire couriers from a variety of sources and social strata. They are more frequently drawn from sailors of the merchant marine. Next to the sailors come the couriers recruited from among the flying personnel of commercial air lines who crisscross the world in every direction. The most valued of them are the pilots themselves. Then comes the category of real and sham business agents who travel in behalf of their companies.

Women play an active part in that branch of service. A number of them have been drawn from the communist milieu among whom there were quite a few divorced wives of foreign communist bigwigs. Men and women of American nationality are favored most for the courier service because their American passports open for them the door to many countries without the need to ask for visas, and, besides, Americans have come to be regarded so much as world travelers that the immigration officers of European and Asiatic countries are not surprised at all if an American lady pops up again and again with her little pet dog on their borders. Foreign journalists, who work for the Soviet intelligence, are often used as unscheduled couriers. And because the journalistic profession serves as an excellent cover for worldwide travel, many underground couriers, who had never had anything to do with journalism, travel under the guise of newspaper correspondents with false credentials from well-known and unknown publications.

When the courier arrives at his destination, he calls up the respective "letter drop," delivers the package, and picks up the mail, if any, for the return journey. The Soviet intelligence maintains a large network of such points in many countries, especially in large ports. The "letter drops" are not encumbered by any organizational forms and do not require a special cover or camouflage. The "letter drop" receives the mail once or twice a month, hides it until an authorized person, with proper credentials and password, comes to pick it up. The person who takes care of the "letter drop" is not obliged to be in attendance the whole day. It is enough for him or her to be near the phone for two hours daily.

Couriers prefer "letter drops" located in stores, restaurants, offices, and other places of business because these are open all day. An owner of a delicatessen store can manage the "letter drop" business by devoting to it not more than a few hours a month. The principal requirement is that the persons in charge of the "letter drops" should be politically reliable and scrupulously honest.

As a rule, new couriers and persons in charge of "letter drops" are subjected, without their knowledge, to a number of tests before real mail is entrusted to their care. For a period of several months they handle dummy packages which do not contain any mail. Later, the packages are examined in a laboratory to determine whether those who handled them made any attempts to look into them. Occasionally, a package is fashioned to look like a solid bundle of dollar bills, and there were a few instances when sailors were tempted to steal the "money" which was not there. Realizing that they have been trapped, the culprits drop out of the service as quietly as possible. Some of them try to repair the damage by resealing the packages, but their crude efforts cannot save them from exposure. As a matter of fact, real money is often forwarded in the same way, but I have never heard of any theft.

There is one more line of communications designed especially to meet the rigorous requirements of wartime intelligence on the territory of the enemy. As is known, an intelligence agent captured in the rear of the enemy lines is not considered a prisoner of war. There are no laws which can protect him. All means, including torture, are employed to break his will and extort from him the names and whereabouts of the other members of the ring. The end is death before a firing squad.

Human endurance is limited, and no one can be sure of his own (or anyone else's) capacity to withstand prolonged physical torture. Thus, the arrest of one man may spell ruin to all his accomplices. Such a situation has driven the chiefs of the Soviet intelligence to seek a way to reduce personal contact among the members of the same ring to the bare minimum and to organize intelligence operations in such a manner that the majority of the agents who take part in the same operation should not know one another, should not meet, and should not know each other's addresses. The idea behind it was, that if a man does not know something he will not be able to divulge it. To comprehend the scheme, as the Soviet intelligence chiefs envisaged it, one must imagine an orchestra consisting of blindfolded musicians brought together in a dark room and playing the same piece without knowing or seeing each other.

How can one speak to another without each seeing the other, how can one contact the other without knowing the other's address? These were the difficulties which had to be overcome. Finally, the KGB intelligence chiefs came up with a plan that had been partly borrowed from the Intelligence Department of the Red Army. It contained the following features:

1) Coded messages take the place of personal talks.

2) Hiding places, such as a hollow in a tree (a cache, in Russian intelligence lingo, *"doubok"*), or a deep crack in the wall of a building, or a hole bored in a public monument, take the place of mailing addresses.

3) A special system of "indicators" is used to orient each agent as to the specific hiding place where a message is awaiting him and where he should deposit collected information. The "indicator" consists of a

number or a symbol written on a wall, park bench, or somewhere inside a railway station, post office, or public telephone booth.

4) Every agent appears on certain days, at a certain hour at a pay telephone booth, where he is called up by his superior and given general instructions.

Thus, according to this plan, an agent takes a walk in the city, looks up the number of the hiding place marked on the wall of a certain building, then goes to that hiding place and, if the coast is clear, picks up the message, deposits his material, and later returns to wipe off the number of the hiding place on the wall and replace it with a cross to show that he has already picked up the message. In case of a misunderstanding, or complication which cannot be cleared up through an exchange of messages, the agent avails himself of the forthcoming "pay telephone" conversation with his superior.

Sometimes, together with the messages, a bundle of money is deposited for the agent, or, if the sum of money is too large, buried in a prearranged spot somewhere in a suburban forest, where the proper agent will later dig it up.

During the last war, in which this system was tried out, still another innovation was added by the KGB intelligence. It consisted of tiny magnetic steel boxes which attach themselves firmly to metal objects. Such a little box, with microfilms inside it, can be stuck on a telegraph pole or post office box, to be picked up later by the proper agent.

The whole system of blind co-operation by phantom agents who do not see each other is far from ideal. A conspiratorial message or a bundle of money left to be picked up by an agent in a crack of a wall or a hollow of a tree can be washed out by a torrential rain or dragged out by squirrels, and if this happens in public view it may attract the attention of the authorities. Burying money in a forest—or digging it up—may accidentally be observed by a chance stroller whose presence is hidden by the trees and bushes. If we examine the pros and cons of this system, we will have to come to the conclusion that for wartime conditions it may have some merits. But for times of peace, with few exceptions, personal contacts between agents are not only preferable but indispensable.

XIV. Chinks in the Agent's Armor

When an underground resident, or another member of the *residentura,* suddenly discovers that he is being shadowed or that his mail has been tampered with, he knows that the government security agencies are after him. This is the time when he must think fast, assess the situation, and make instantaneous decisions concerning himself and the safety of his associates and the members of the network. The officer cancels or drops his appointments, destroys all documentary and material vestiges of his conspiratorial work, and takes a number of other steps provided for emergency situations. Whether the officer withdraws temporarily into a hide-out until things have cleared up, or flees the country, the disturbing questions inevitably arise: What has prompted the police to put him under surveillance? How much do the police know about him? Could it be that there is a traitor within the Soviet network? Have the police succeeded in trailing the officer to his meetings with other members of the ring? Many other questions demand an immediate answer. Only when the *residentura* is manned by highly qualified officers, who strictly observe the conspiratorial rules of intelligence and operate with clocklike precision, can the trouble spot be quickly found. Otherwise, the *residentura* may be demobilized for a long time by fears and doubts extending in every direction.

The search for the trouble spot or weak link within the intelligence organization can be likened to the checking of a break in the electric wiring of a warship. All the components of the *residentura* with its broad network of informants are carefully re-examined, analyzed, and secretly tested. But sometimes the most minute check-up will not reveal the cause of the trouble for the simple reason that it may lie outside the sphere of the intelligence organization and its operations. The cause may be hidden in the private lives of the intelligence officers with their personal weaknesses and transgressions, which in the unsafe conditions of the underground may involve them in trouble. I have in mind first of all romantic attachments in which some Russian intelligence officers get themselves entangled as a result of their longing to find relief from the tense and lonely life in the grim atmosphere of the underground.

This is a serious problem. The history of the KGB underground knows quite a few cases in which an intelligence officer, while on a protracted assignment in a foreign land, fell in love with a woman who had no idea of her lover's real identity, occupation, or even nationality. There were instances, though rare ones, when such romantic attachments led to matrimony and the disruption of a previous marriage.

Infatuated girls tend to close their eyes to strange discrepancies that may transpire in the life story and behavior of the man they love, but their parents worry over the future of their daughters. When parents see that their daughter has seriously involved herself with a foreigner, they want to know more about him and make sure that he is an honorable man, at least not a bigamist, and that he will be able to support a wife and family. The parents are prone to start a little investigation of their own, sometimes through the good offices of the pastor of their church, who writes to his counterpart in the other country, and sometimes through the family lawyer and even through a regular detective's office. This is the juncture at which the fireworks are likely to erupt, as can be seen from the following story.

One Soviet resident who was working in the underground in Hitler's Germany, where he posed as a Canadian, was tipped off by the elevator man of his apartment house that a detective had come to the house and made inquiries about him. The news came as a shock. The resident was in the midst of an important recruiting operation of great potentialities. Was there a connection between both things? Could it be that the Gestapo had outwitted him and smoked him out of his shell with tempting bait? According to the way the recruitment had originated and developed, this looked most improbable. But what was it that caused the detective's visit?

In the meantime, all precautionary measures, prescribed for such occasions, were taken. A warning was sent out to the other members of the *residenturas*. Each officer checked and rechecked all his possessions to eliminate and destroy everything that tended to compromise him. Several projects were put off. New channels for emergency communications were set up. The resident left the city ostensibly on business, but in reality he repaired to the estate of a wealthy but reliable friend of Russia which was considered a safe haven. All his energy was now concentrated on finding the source of the leak which led to the detective's visit. Moscow was duly informed about the situation. The resident hoped to find the key to the mystery through an informant who worked at the Gestapo. However, the clarification came from entirely unexpected quarters: from Moscow itself.

The resident, who was posing in Berlin as a Canadian businessman from Montreal, had a love affair with a young German girl. Seeing how seriously she was infatuated with the foreigner, the parents of the girl decided to check up on their prospective son-in-law and instructed a German private detective to find out everything possible about the beau of their daughter and about his family in Canada. Accordingly, the German detective wrote to a well-known detective bureau in Montreal. The Canadian detective approached the sister of our Canadian businessman. She was greatly surprised when the detective inquired about her younger brother Joseph, who had been killed in an accident some fifteen years back. She assured the detective that he was on the wrong track and that the man in Berlin was not her brother. About two weeks later the detective came to her again. He was puzzled by strange coincidences and asked her to help him unravel the mystery. As it has turned out, the Joseph who lived in Berlin was born on the same day as her late brother and attended the same preparatory school in Toronto. The detective told her also that two years earlier a Canadian passport had been issued in Ottawa to her brother's double and that in his application he had named a certain Julius as his brother. Did she know Julius?—Of course, she did. Julius was her older brother, a lawyer. The woman was shocked and hurried with the detective to the office of her brother. The brother listened to the story in amazement and said he could not figure it out. However, as soon as the detective left, the brother, who was privy to the whole affair, got in touch with the Soviet embassy and warned the "comrades" that their man in Berlin was in serious trouble. The Soviet legal resident at the embassy cabled the story to Moscow, and Moscow wired to the underground resident in Berlin that he should get out of Germany at once.

There is one other area in which underground officers display impermissible lightmindedness and an amazing disregard of their own safety. As has been made clear in these pages, one of the main preoccupations of the underground officer is to protect his fraudulently acquired identity from exposure. A lot of spade work goes into the selection and acquisition of a false passport for the officer. Much ingenuity is applied to invent a plausible biography and build a secure business cover for him. Years of training have been spent to make a skillful operative of him and to instill in him the importance of vigilance in the conspiratorial craft of intelligence. And yet, all caution is suddenly thrown to the wind the moment the underground officer buys an automobile! It is enough for a curious informant or a police detective, who tries to pick up the trail of the Russian agent, to catch sight of the automobile license plates, and he can quickly get a lowdown on the Soviet officer, including his name, address, nationality, and so on. It was in this way that one underground resident was tracked down and arrested by the German Gestapo after a Western journalist, who had known him in Russia as an NKVD chief, jotted down the number of his license plates and turned it over to the police. After that incident the head of the NKVD warned the underground residents that for them to drive a car in a foreign country was tantamount to inscribing their names and addresses on their foreheads for everyone to see. But the admonition was largely disregarded. Soviet officers proved simply unable to resist the temptation of enjoying the convenience of a personal car, and Moscow could not—and did not really try hard enough to—enforce its ban. Gradually, a compromise of sorts was worked out. Underground officers were forbidden to ride in their cars to meeting places with informants and were advised to avoid as much as possible using their cars in the city proper. To decrease the chance of being recognized while driving in populated areas, the officers began to don caps and dark glasses, but these things are, of course, ineffectual expedients.

Still another weakness in the psychological make-up of the underground resident leads him to violate one of the cardinal rules of security. This weakness stems from the lonely life he lives in a hostile environment of a foreign land, away from his family, friends, and country. According to security rules, underground residents are strictly forbidden to associate with anyone from the local Soviet embassy or with other underground residents who happen to operate, or visit, in the same area. However, being eager to learn the latest news from home and to have an intimate talk with a friend or colleague, the residents often violate the rule when an opportunity to see someone from the KGB intelligence presents itself.

In some countries, residents began to meet each other at regular intervals and formed a sort of clearinghouse where they exchanged news from home, intelligence shoptalk, and gossip. This was kept a secret from Moscow. However, in 1935 two scandalous incidents took place which put an end to these transgressions. The more serious one occurred in Germany, when one evening an NKVD underground resident was entertaining two of his friends in his flat—the underground resident in Prague, who had arrived in Berlin for a few days, and an attaché of the Soviet embassy in Berlin, who was the NKVD legal resident in Germany. While the three friends were sipping coffee and enjoying an interesting conversation, the doorbell rang out rather shrilly, and three young Gestapo officers appeared. They asked permission to inspect the premises and wanted to see the identification papers of those present. The men produced their passports: one had a Soviet diplomatic passport, the second a Swedish, and the third a Czechoslovakian. The officers jotted down the names, copied a few details from the Soviet passport and left. When the two Russian guests attempted to leave, they found that the exit from the house was blocked and that the street was full of police cars. They had to return to their friend's flat.

The next day the Russian tenant of the flat learned from his neighbors that the Gestapo agents had inspected in the same way all the apartments in the whole block. Either the Gestapo was looking for somebody, or this was a Nazi exercise in mass searches. Whichever it was, it looked unpleasant. Such a thing could not be concealed from Headquarters, and Moscow recalled both underground residents.

Another typical transgression nurtured by the same feeling of homesickness and nostalgia consisted of the habit of underground officers of keeping letters received from their families back home (which arrive in the form of microfilms) for long periods of time, instead of destroying them after reading them. Many underground officers are simply unable to part with such missives, especially if they have been scribbled by their little children. I have seen such a letter, shown to me by one of the bravest, and I thought toughest, men I had ever known. The letter had a contour drawing of a little child's hand with an inscription in Russian, obviously made by the mother. It read: "Daddy, see how big my hand is now. I shall be two years old tomorrow. I already walk and talk. Please, daddy, come home. Your little Ninochka." The officer's eyes welled with tears. He kept the snapshot with the imprint of his child's hand in his wallet as a kind of talisman and did not want to destroy it, come what might.

And yet, there were instances when the discovery of such a photo-letter during the arrest of an underground operative on a charge of espionage served to confirm the allegation of the prosecution that the arrested man was a Russian and conducted his espionage work in behalf of the Soviet Union. For that reason, most of the underground *residenturas* conduct their correspondence with Moscow not in Russian but in some foreign language. Moscow, on its part, follows suit. In accordance with security regulations, the resident and his officers do not keep secret documents in their possession a minute longer than necessary to get them under way through secret channels to Moscow. The only exception which some residents make at their own peril and in defiance of the security rules is that, when they send to Moscow each month a detailed financial account of the *residentura's* expenses, they retain a photocopy of the account until they have received a confirmation from Moscow that the account had been approved. Since it takes about a month to get the confirmation from Headquarters, the keeping of a photocopy of the *residentura's* expenses twelve months a year is a risky matter, as one NKVD resident learned to his sorrow when the Italian secret police apprehended him and his wife in Milan with the financial records of the *residentura* in their possession. However, even after this debacle in Italy, the financial data continued to be kept by two leading residents who did not see eye to eye with the NKVD intelligence chiefs on matters of intelligence policy and who were afraid that the financial accounts they forwarded to Moscow might be maliciously "mislaid" there, in which case they might be confronted, many months later, with a demand to account for some twenty thousand dollars in past expenses. The two resident directors apparently mistrusted their own chiefs more than they feared the chiefs of the foreign counterspy agencies.

XV. Guerrilla Warfare

In chapter II, defining the basic lines of activity of the KGB Intelligence, I pointed out that the KGB was also in charge of Guerrilla Warfare.

Although by its very nature guerrilla operations ought to have been under the command of the Red Army, this branch of warfare was since the days of the Russian Civil War so closely interrelated with intelligence operations that it has been recognized as the responsibility of the organs of the KGB.

There are two major types of guerrilla wars: One is a war of *national liberation* waged by bands of the civilian population against a foreign invader. The other is an armed struggle of an outraged segment of the people *against the injustices of the internal regime*. The fierce struggle which had been waged by bands of Russian peasants against the invading armies of Napoleon in 1812 may serve as an example of the first type of guerrilla warfare. The rebellion of the Cuban farmers against the oppressive regime of Fulgencio Batista is a classic example of the second type. We are witnessing now new attempts by disillusioned Cubans to organize guerrilla resistance to the totalitarian regime of Castro.

During the first phases of its development, the guerrilla force is infinitely smaller and weaker than the forces of the oppressive regime inside the country.

Whereas the armies of the government may comprise tens of thousands of troops, with artillery, tanks, and aircraft, the burgeoning guerrilla force may consist of but a few hundred poorly armed men who would be wiped out in a matter of hours, had they not had two significant and far-reaching advantages: (1) the support of the local population and (2) the inaccessibility of their fortress-like refuge in the mountains or in the forests. I have put the support of the local population ahead of the inaccessible sanctuary because the history of guerrilla warfare has shown that without the help of the population guerrilla fighters are doomed, whereas, if the terrain where they operate has no natural defenses, they still can hide behind the people and, if hopelessly surrounded, dissolve themselves among the population. During the Russian Civil War, the guerrillas led by the Ukrainian nationalist and anarchist Makhno, who fought both the Reds and the Whites, played hide and seek with the punitive expeditions of his enemies, but when surrounded they would hide their rifles and assume the appearance of peaceful peasants tilling the field, tending the horses or mending the roofs. The pursuers would be told by the inhabitants that a guerrilla band of about so many men had just passed hurriedly by and made its way through this or that ravine or to the reed-covered banks of the river.

Peaceful peasants and other groups of hard-working people do not take up arms so lightly against superior forces of the government, unless they have been driven to it by unendurable hardships, onerous taxation, property confiscations, and naked violence. Before armed resistance succeeds in gaining land reforms and concessions from greedy landlords and corrupt government, peaceful life is disrupted, the rural economy is disorganized, trade is at a standstill, whole communities are devastated, and lives are destroyed. It is because the injustices and sufferings have reached the boiling point that the most desperate and determined men take whatever weapons they can lay their hands on—from fowling pieces to axes and clubs—and retire into the hills and the woods, from where they stage fierce raids on the estates of their feudal overlords and local police outposts. The men become outlaws. The authority of the government is defied. Punitive detachments of rural police arrive to track them down. People suspected of aiding the rebels are persecuted. Many are arrested. Order is gradually restored. The authorities learn from the population that the outlaws have fled to another county. But when everything seems quiet and the detachments are getting ready to depart, the rebels come down from the hills in the middle of the night, overwhelm the sentries, destroy the police force, and make away with their rifles and ammunition. The population begins to regard the guerrilla band not only as a fighting unit, but also as a political entity united by the ideal of freeing the inhabitants from the arbitrary rule of the landlords and their feudalistic regime.

Before long, army units arrive to quell the rebellion. Martial law is proclaimed. The troops invade the hills, are drawn deeper into them by the retreating rebels until the soldiers find themselves before an inaccessible mountain position, from behind which the rebels cut them down with rifle fire and homemade grenades. Beaten and exhausted, the surviving soldiers return to their quarters. The rebels pick up the rifles, machine guns, and ammunition of the fallen men. The guerrilla war is now on . . .

The rebels live off the land. The local population supports them with food, clothes, footwear, and above all with accurate intelligence. The guerrillas know of every move made by the troops, their exact strength and location, and the arrival of reinforcements. On the other hand, the government troops are hampered by the complete inability to obtain information about the movements of the guerrillas and are often misled altogether by misinformation. The command of the troops resents the silent co-operation between the population and the rebels and begins to apply repressive measures toward the inhabitants. As a result, many of the younger people flee to the hills, thus swelling the number of the guerrillas. The inability of the government to quash the rebellion and the daring forays staged by the guerrillas make for their popularity. The guerrilla war grows and spreads to the adjoining districts.

One of the basic principles of guerrilla strategy is to inflict the maximum of casualties on the adversary with minimum loss to the rebels. To achieve this the guerrillas should never accept battle with superior enemy forces. They must offset the superiority of the enemy by cunning planning, deception, and even outright perfidy. They must hit the enemy where and when least expected and, having administered a stunning blow, disengage themselves before the enemy has had time to recover and regroup for a counterblow. They must make good use of their familiarity with the terrain to harass the enemy during the night and to intercept and attack his moving columns on the roads. They must plant false informers for the purpose of deceiving the enemy and luring him into prearranged traps.

Surprise, mobility, sharp attacks, and quick withdrawals are the principles of guerrilla tactics. The guerrillas must seek engagements with the enemy under conditions of their own choosing and concentrate the attack on the enemy's rear and flanks. The motto of the guerrilla strategists is: "Our front is their (the enemy's) rear." Guerrillas must harass the enemy continually and terrorize him especially at night, making him feel that guerrillas lurk behind every bush. How effective a night operation can be, may be seen from the following incident that took place in Spain during the Civil War in the 1930's.

A squad of fifteen guerrillas armed with hand grenades, single shot carbines, and a few tommy guns stole toward an enemy army column of about 400 men encamped for the night near the road, some thirty miles behind the front line. The troops arrived with an assignment to combat the Republican guerrillas on a sector of the front which had been inactive for over two months and which was favored by the guerrillas for crossings into enemy territory. The guerrillas crawled toward the camp, Indian fashion, from two sides. One sentry was disposed of in silence. The other was nowhere to be seen and was probably fast asleep. Then, two Molotov cocktails were thrown at the tents, which ignited and lit up the whole area. About a dozen hand grenades were immediately thrown into the tents as the soldiers ran out completely bewildered by the roaring explosions. Only a few of them had guns in their hands, and they shot right and left at their own men. A few more grenades were flung into the band of panicked men. Many lay dead and wounded. Some of the men ran into the path of the guerrillas and were picked off by single carbine shots. The guerrillas withdrew without suffering a single casualty.

Guerrillas do not fight to seize real estate. They do not capture or defend fixed positions as do regular army units in conventional wars. Were they to try to do so, they would be surrounded by superior forces and annihilated. Until the guerrillas have succeeded in evolving into a big military force organized along regular army lines, their role must be limited to harassing and weakening the enemy by wiping out his small columns, bothering the big ones, attacking his bases and arsenals, plundering his supply convoys, disrupting his lines of communications, upsetting his operations, and forcing him to divert considerable forces in order to protect his every step. A thing which is considered despicable in the regular army, such as running away from the enemy, is not a shameful act at all in guerrilla warfare. On the contrary, the guerrilla fighter is trained to run fast and is encouraged to kill as many enemies as he can by a surprise assault and to run for his life, because the motto of the guerrilla fighters is: *"Kill the enemy and survive yourself."*

The guerrillas must guard the approaches to their own base day and night. Avenues to the base must be blocked by obstacles, escape routes kept open. A sufficient number of men must be on guard duty at all times. Only especially selected men should have access to the stores of ammunition and supplies. The constant presence of a physician must be secured and, if a doctor cannot be persuaded to join the guerrillas, he must be drafted against his will. Guerrillas must also secure the help of other physicians in the near-by settlements and arrange to have a certain number of beds in a hospital or private homes. Medical supplies are obtained principally from the ambushed supply columns of the enemy.

As new volunteers and men fleeing from police persecution flock to the guerrilla camp, new guerrilla units are formed under the command of veterans, and new bases are established. The new outfits carry out their raids independently of each other, but they must coordinate their daily operations and divide the targets among themselves in order not to blunder at night into armed clashes with each other.

Loyalty and comradeship are the cement that holds guerrillas together. A comrade should never be abandoned in distress. A good commander must see to it that conflicts and quarrels arising among his men should be resolved before they cause serious damage. The members of the outfit must be well indoctrinated as to the purpose of the struggle and their responsibility to the population and the nation as a whole. Many guerrillas have a tendency to think that if they fight in defense of the rights of the people, they are entitled to gratuities from the people. Some of the men go so far as to "confiscate," in the name of the guerrilla unit, things which they covet for themselves. Such abuses, if widely practiced, may alienate the population and cause great harm. It is impossible to hold a guerrilla band in line without rigorous discipline. Misdemeanors and moral transgressions are best dealt with by a "Comradely Court," elected by the members of the gang. Serious breaches of discipline must be dealt with by the commander himself. Treason, if it has been proved beyond any doubt, is punished by death.

If the majority of the population consists of poor farmers and the country is very small and if the guerrillas have competent political leaders, the chances are that the guerrilla operations will culminate in a triumphant revolution. However, if the country is large and possesses a fairly developed industry and a strong middle class, the government will succeed in blockading and quarantining the guerrilla area until the impoverished population is no longer able to sustain the guerrilla fighters. Punitive expeditions will finally stamp out the rebellion. Partial concessions and reforms will then be introduced to pacify the area.

Whereas intelligence operations are conducted by the organs of the KGB continually in time of peace and in time of war, guerrilla operations are carried out only in wartime and in semiwar situations. The organs of the KGB were in the guerrilla business as early as 1919–20, during the Russian Civil War and the Russo-Polish War of the same period. The operations of the guerrilla detachments against the Poles consisted mainly of infiltrating the rear of the enemy and staging night raids on the headquarters of Polish army units, killing the commanders, and making off with army maps, war plans and other data concerning the strength and disposition of the Polish forces. Occasionally, the guerrilla detachments succeeded in bringing back to the Soviet side a "tongue"—a captured Polish staff officer who could disclose additional information. On one such occasion, a Soviet guerrilla outfit captured the commander of all the Polish guerrilla forces, Colonel Senkovsky, who had arrived at the front to supervise the crossing to the Russian side of about forty Polish officers and Savinkov [1] agents who were given the assignment to head a force of about

---

1 Boris Savinkov, famous Russian revolutionary and terrorist who helped the French, British, and Polish general staffs to fight the Soviet state with subversion.

8000 Ukrainian anti-Soviet rebels and deserters who hid in the forests and to strike at the rear of the Twelfth Red Army, which was at that time in full retreat. The other important task of the Soviet guerrilla detachments in the Russo-Polish War was to disrupt the enemy's communications by blowing up bridges, railway tracks, power installations, and telephone and telegraph lines. As a rule, Soviet guerrillas act as an auxiliary force and co-ordinate their operations with those of the regular army.

The experience gained by the Soviet guerrilla troops in the Russo-Polish War became the cornerstone of the Soviet guerrilla science of the future. Sixteen years later, in 1936, during the Spanish Civil War, the former commander of the Soviet guerrilla troops in the Russo-Polish War was sent by the Russian Politburo to Spain, where he organized and directed for the Republican government of Spain guerrilla detachments which operated in the rear of Franco's forces.

The guerrilla operations in Spain began in a rather modest way with the organization of two saboteur schools for about two hundred men each, one in Madrid and the other in Benimamet, near Valencia. Later, four more schools were added, one of which, in Barcelona, numbered six hundred men. The trainees were young Spaniards, selected from the Republican Army, with a sprinkling of German communists from the International Brigade and about eighty former Russian tsarist officers who hoped to earn the right to return to their motherland. They were trained principally in various kinds of demolition work, high-grade marksmanship, elementary guerrilla tactics (raids and ambushes), map reading, living off the land, and long marches with loads up to twenty-five pounds. On graduation each trainee had to be able to plan and execute the demolition (on contact or by remote control) of various types of bridges, railway tracks, and power lines, and to mine roads.

The saboteurs, in groups of seven or nine, would cross into enemy territory by night on an inactive sector of the front with well-defined assignments. Each commando unit would set out for its destination, carefully by-passing inhabited points, walking by night, and hiding and resting by day. The commandos would blow up a bridge or mine the railway track and wait for the military train to pass. They would watch the explosion and the resultant wreck from a distance, hiding in the grass, bushes, or rocks. Knowing that an army emergency squad would arrive at the scene, the saboteurs would mine the road some two hundred yards from the train wreck, and when the troop-carrying trucks were on the fatal spot they would be blown up. Mission accomplished, the commandos would then return to the Republican side. The recrossing of the front into Republican territory was not a simple operation and had to be carefully prepared. According to instructions, the saboteurs had to approach the Republican front line at a certain spot and give a pre-arranged signal so that they should not be fired upon. They had to be careful not to err to the right or left of the prearranged crossing point. The army battalion at that sector would be warned not to shoot at a little group of men expected to come from the enemy territory in all probability during the night or at daybreak. Sometimes the saboteurs would be prevented from returning to the prearranged line because during their absence that line would suddenly become alive with action and counteraction and they would have to look for a quieter crossing place and take a chance that the uninformed soldiers would take a few potshots at them. The commandos would usually send ahead one man with a white flag. There was a standard joke among the guerrillas that this man would do well to recite the well-known prayer: "O, Lord, save me from my friends. From my enemies I will protect myself."

Gradually, the incursions became routine and saboteur groups began to make inroads into the enemy's territory on a wide front. On the Madrid sector alone, not fewer than five teams crossed into the enemy's rear every night, and after the first three months of operation at least 40 per cent of the bridges and power lines, within sixty kilometers from the front, were down. The enemy was seriously disturbed, and special army units were assigned to combat the new menace of "Marxist guerrilleros," as they were referred to in General Franco's orders.

The Republican guerrilla force grew fast, and by the summer of 1937 its operations became more sophisticated. Guerrilla commandos had assignments not only to destroy lines of communications but to harass the enemy deeper in his territory by attacking arsenals and ambushing moving columns and supply convoys. To do that, more detailed information was needed as to the location of the enemy garrisons and arsenals and the movements of his troops. For that purpose Republican army units were searched for men whose families lived in the territory occupied by the Nationalists within 150 kilometers from the front. These men were transferred from the army to the guerrilla troops, and after a short intensive course of training and indoctrination they were sent to visit their families and, where possible, to stay with them and collect the necessary intelligence. Thus, assisted by inside knowledge, a group of some fifty guerrillas (a platoon) would swoop down in the middle of the night on the garrison barracks, housing ten times as many men, and pelt them with hand grenades, incendiary bombs, and machine gun fire, completely paralyzing their ability to resist and inflicting heavy casualties on them. Then, faithfully following the guerrilla tradition, the attackers would suddenly withdraw and disappear into the night. At the same time, other groups were attacking other targets elsewhere.

One night, an enemy supply convoy of twelve trucks was ambushed and destroyed some 120 kilometers inside the enemy rear. Two or three of the trucks were loaded with canned food. Considering the acute shortage of food in the country, it was quite natural for the inhabitants of near-by villages to help themselves to the cans that were scattered along the road. In the morning, an army detachment arrived. The military police searched the homes in the village nearest to the scene, and in some of them found cans and a few army blankets stolen from the ambushed convoy. The military authorities regarded this as sufficient proof of the existence of collusion between the inhabitants and the guerrillas. A number of people were arrested and some beaten up. The younger men took to the hills. Some of them made their way to Republican territory, but the majority remained and turned into rebels. The Republican guerrillas dispatched instructors to them, large Mauser pistols, and Nationalist currency.

Similar incidents occurred in many other places, and everywhere the suspicion of the Nationalists fell on the local population, because the sympathies of the poor peasants and the workers for the Republican cause was unmistakenly clear. The wider the guerrilla operations spread, the stronger the suspicion grew that the population was aiding the saboteurs. Reprisals by the military were quick and severe.

One morning, a guerrilla squad of seven men had just blown up a power line and settled down behind rocks to wait for the army repair crew to arrive. In the meantime, four men, who were passing by on their way to the railway station, a kilometer away, approached the scene. Two of them wore military attire, each with a small suitcase in his hand. While they were standing there, contemplating the wreckage, a repair crew and M.P.'s approached. The commandos refrained from blowing them up by remote control for fear of harming the bystanders. The first thing the M.P.'s did was to arrest and search the four men. Then the crew examined the damage and the party left. About ten days later, an announcement appeared in every village along the route, informing the people that four brothers, two of them artillerymen, who had been on furlough in their village, were courtmartialed and shot for blowing up a power line.

Soon acts of repressions spread to other districts, and the rural population became restive. This afforded the guerrilla high command an opportunity to send experienced agitators to several workers' regions with instructions to prepare the ground for guerrilla activities on a broader scale. These attempts were especially successful in the region of Río Tinto and Aroche, about 350 kilometers deep in enemy territory, where one of the world's biggest copper mines is situated. The first operations were carried out there by squads of saboteurs dispatched from Republican Spain. The local authorities reacted to these acts of sabotage with reprisals against the miners. This caused many miners to flee to the hills. That was the beginning of a long and highly successful guerrilla campaign. The miners, handy with dynamite by virtue of their occupation, quickly mastered the art of demolition and began to blow up bridges, ammunition dumps, and lines of communication. Government troops sent to suppress the guerrillas were unable to clear the hills of them. On the contrary, assisted by information from the inhabitants, the guerrillas succeeded in ambushing and routing the punitive detachments sent to suppress them. The government answered with repressive measures against the families of the fighting miners, and this embittered the rebels still further. It was like a wave against wave, whipping up the passions on both sides. The Río Tinto guerrilla force grew fast and soon numbered three thousand men. But it lacked two important things: competent leaders and suitable weapons. The high command of the Republican guerrillas hastened to provide both. A staff of experienced Spanish saboteurs led by two Soviet experts in guerrilla warfare, Major Strik and Captain S. Glushko, was dispatched to Río Tinto. They made their way there on foot through hundreds of kilometers of enemy territory without incident. They took with them a supply of Nationalist currency and two-way radio transmitters. As soon as the two Russians reached their destination, they selected a suitable site on which Soviet bombers soon dropped the first supply of weapons, which consisted of hundreds of tommy guns, German large automatic Mausers, light carbines, and hand grenades. The Russians stayed for four months, training men in actual combat. One of them, Stepan Glushko, was killed in action. By that time, one Spaniard who combined in himself qualities of a leader with idealism and rare courage had become the commander of the Río Tinto rebels. His name was Dr. Moro, a local physician who had joined the guerrillas voluntarily. Dr. Moro was killed in the spring of 1938 while leading an attack on an enemy arsenal, in which thousands of fully fused artillery shells were blown up.

In 1937 the air forces of both sides in the Spanish Civil War fought for supremacy in the skies. Many breathtaking duels were taking place in clear, sunny weather over Madrid, in view of the public. It was like a colossal circus, with the blue sky as the dome and the people watching from beneath with bated breath to see which of the flying gladiators in the shiny armor of his plane would plummet to death. On the one side there were Spanish and Russian fliers, on the other Spanish and German. Spaniards against Spaniards— this was the essence of the civil conflict. Russians against Germans was the preview of the Russo-German war that was soon to unfold. Guerrillas do not fly planes, but they can do their part in the war against the enemy air force. Spain was the first country in which guerrillas showed that they could fight the battle of the skies on the ground.

The first exploits in this field were carried out by a Spanish guerrilla band under the command of an outstanding Soviet guerrilla fighter, Captain Nicolayevsky. In all his operations he would first gather detailed intelligence on the number of bombers, fighter planes, and men on the enemy air field, the location of the hangars, if any, of the gasoline tanks, of the barracks housing the pilots and ground personnel, and of the position of sentries on duty. His methods of attack varied. Sometimes he would sneak up to the air field, demobilize the sentries, and assign each of his three squads to specific tasks. One squad would take care of the bombers and the gasoline tanks, another of the barracks, a third of the fighter planes, and so on. Then, at a given signal, hell would descend on the field. The bomber and fighter planes would be blown up and burned, and the gasoline tanks ignited.

At other times his operations were more sophisticated, with a touch of a movie plot in them. In the summer of 1937 he carried out two such assaults within five days. In one of them Nicolayevsky and his men, bearing the insignia of the Nationalist army, sneaked under cover of darkness to the vicinity of the military air field. There he requisitioned two passing military trucks, and the whole gang rode straight to the field. Nicolayevsky was a blond giant and would never be mistaken for a Spaniard. But he could easily pass as a German and, for that reason, he fixed a large swastika band on his arm. They rode past the open-mouthed sentries without stopping, shouting the Fascist slogan "Arriba España" and drove up to the main building. There, Nicolayevsky's Spanish assistant introduced himself to the officer on duty as Captain So-and-so of a certain Franco division, on a special mission, and asked to arrange for them a place to sleep for the remainder of the night. He flashed before the officer his forged identity papers. The officer on duty obliged and sent an orderly to show the men to a barrack-like structure beside a huge hangar. On the way there, they saw a few silhouettes of large-winged bombers. A dozen or so men slept on the bunks in the barracks. This was a perfect replica of the Trojan horse story. Because of the utter darkness, it was impossible to make out the layout of the field and the disposition of the big birds, and Nicolayevsky decided to wait for the first signs of daybreak.

Finally, when pale light began to filter through to the field, they saw opposite the barracks a new two-story building which, they knew, housed the pilots. Not far away was a row of big bombers. And farther in the field one could make out through the morning mist small clusters of tiny fighter planes. From this moment it was already routine for the battle-hardened guerrillas. Nicolayevsky gave the signal and pandemonium broke loose. Within an hour the band was on its way back to the Republican territory. The cost to the attackers: two lightly wounded guerrillas.

The last heroic exploit accomplished by Nicolayevsky was his attack on a military air field, sixty kilometers from the port of Almería, the southernmost tip of Republican-held territory. He was killed outright, not by the enemy, but by his own hand grenade which exploded prematurely when he swung his arm back to throw it at a group of resisting pilots.

On the way to their targets, the guerrilla commandos were always careful to bypass enemy check points on the roads, and for that reason they were often obliged to take long roundabout hikes over rugged terrain to get to a point which otherwise would have been a simple matter to reach. This often interfered with the time available for the operation, especially in the summer, when the guerrillas had only five hours of darkness to leave their hiding place, make their way to the target, carry out the operation, and move as far as possible from the scene of destruction. To overcome these difficulties the Guerrilla Command began to furnish the commandos with forged identification and assignment papers in which they figured as outfits of some enemy unit, ostensibly on a special mission. The men, of course, had to be able to name the location of the unit to which they allegedly belonged. These identification papers came in handy also in cases when a guerrilla outfit stumbled unexpectedly on an enemy patrol. Instead of shooting it out, the guerrillas merely produced their papers.

One Spanish commander of a guerrilla platoon devised a way to overcome still another, no less vexing predicament. His outfit had an assignment to blow up an enemy arsenal which, according to intelligence reports, had twenty-four security guards living on the premises. About a quarter of a mile from the arsenal on the highway there was a check point at which the password was demanded from everyone who wanted to enter the compound of the arsenal and the near-by arms repair shops. The guerrillas did not know the password. If they attempted to shoot their way past the check point, the guards at the arsenal would be alerted and the guerrillas would have had a hot reception. The ingenious commander of the group resorted to a trick that disclosed the secret password to him. He stopped his men at a spot on the highway about a mile from the check point and there formed his own "check point" astride the road. He might have stood there with his outfit the whole night in vain, if nobody had come that way. But luck was with him. In about an hour a truck which belonged to the repair shops drove up. "Password?" demanded the commander. The answer was prompt. "God is with us," said the driver. He was waved on. After that, the commando followed its commander, who wore a lieutenant's insignia of the

Nationalist army, toward the arsenal. They approached the check point whistling a Falangist march tune. "Where are you going?" they were asked.—"To the repair shops," answered the lieutenant. "Password?" —"Why, of course, *God is with us!*" The guerrillas attacked the sleeping guards in their quarters. Then they placed charges under the ammunition boxes and the store of explosives and ran for their lives.

The trick of establishing false check points was later put to other uses as well. Little groups of guerrillas, wearing false insignia, established such points in various enemy districts, stopped military cars, examined the papers of the passengers, and inquired about the location of their units, thus gathering fresh intelligence needed for planning new operations. On one occasion an enemy major, who had a briefcase full of logistics data, and his chauffeur, were ordered out of their car and marched to the Republican side. There the major furnished valuable information on the state of military supplies on the Madrid front.

The lessons of Spain proved invaluable to the Russians in the war against the German invaders. Tens of thousands of "partisans" (the Russian name for guerrillas), organized and led by the KGB guerrilla experts, harassed the German overextended lines of communications from Poland to Stalingrad, from Kiev to the Caucasus, and from Latvia to Leningrad, blowing up bridges and troop trains, mining roads, attacking marching columns, and plundering supplies and ammunition. The basic guerrilla strategy developed during the Russian Civil War and in Spain remained essentially the same, but had to be adapted to operations of colossal dimensions. Swelled by the influx of Russian peasants and city dwellers, many guerrilla bands numbered several thousand each, and, using artillery, mortars, and bazookas seized from the enemy, they were now able to rout battalion-size units of the German army. But the old rules—not to enter into battle against superior forces and not to engage in a war of positions —held good. The basic strategy continued to be that of delivering a lightning blow and disengaging oneself from the enemy in order to get ready to strike the next blow at another place. Harassed, ambushed, and battered at every turn, the Germans found to their sorrow that in Russia the rear was also a fighting front. To get supplies to the German armies across thousands of kilometers of Russian territory had become an almost impossible task. Bridges, rebuilt by the German engineers, were blown up again before they had even been used. Without regular supplies in men and arms, the strength and fighting power of the German armies deep inside Russia could not be sustained. The KGB saboteurs and terrorists roamed the cities in Nazi uniforms with forged credentials and passes. Russian cooks and maidservants, employed in the houses occupied by Hitler's commissioners of occupation, planted bombs in the bedrooms of the German masters and blew them up. The fury of guerrilla warfare was restrained neither by the rules of international conventions nor by humanitarian considerations. Germans captured in guerrilla battles were not given the status of prisoners-of-war and were shot on the spot.

XVI. Evaluation of Information

One of the important functions of intelligence is the evaluation of the information obtained as to its authenticity and political significance. The standard procedure of evaluating the authenticity of a document hinges on the examination of the physical characteristics of the procured material and on the analysis of its content.

The paramount element in evaluating a document, or a piece of oral information, is the degree of reliability of the *source,* through which the information has been obtained. If a completely trustworthy informant brings a document which he lifted from the secret files, the Soviet officer knows it is above suspicion. The same goes for oral information. When a devoted informant, who has always been truthful, says that he has seen or read such and such a report, or transcript of a conference, the intelligence officer knows that this is so.

In cases when the informant has not yet been sufficiently tested, the Soviet intelligence tries to check every scrap of paper, or information, that comes from him. The checking is less difficult when the Soviet intelligence has a parallel informant in the same government office with access to the same files.

It must be said that in the departments of Western governments secret documents are not always guarded well enough, and this neglect has been taken advantage of by the Soviet intelligence. The transcripts of most secret meetings of the government are usually sent out to at least 18–20 dignitaries, each of whom has an office with clerks and secretaries who have or can have access to the material. There were cases when a Western government had become aware that a certain transcript of one of its meetings had fallen into the hands of the Russians. However, it was impossible to ascertain from which of the twenty places the document had been lifted and photographed. Often the Soviet *residentura* in a foreign country receives the same document from two places. This affords the possibility of crosschecking the work of two informants.

The Soviet intelligence is more wary with documents received from informants who are greedy for money, especially in cases where the amount of the reward, or bonus, is geared to the importance of the document. I remember a case, when a fairly valuable informant in Germany, wishing to secure for himself higher pay, claimed that he had read and made brief notes from a draft of a secret treaty which was being negotiated between Japan and Germany. Because the treaty was directed against the Soviet Union, the information created quite a stir in the Kremlin. However, within a month of checking, the *residentura* succeeded in establishing that the informant lied, which he himself finally admitted.

The law of demand and supply manifests itself in intelligence too. Knowing that government agencies seek information and pay well for it, some unscrupulous persons get busy forging "secret" information and offer it to various governments. Some falsifiers who have a knack for international affairs and follow the world press closely are able to fabricate documents which attract the interest of the foreign offices of the world. These characters approach foreign embassies and ministries with their wares, often misrepresenting themselves as go-betweens acting in behalf of "personal friends" in the diplomatic service of another state. Some intelligence services are taken in and begin to acquire the material, only to find out later that they were paying money for outright forgeries. And sometimes they are even unable to get rid of an unscrupulous supplier, because an influential policymaker of the government has found the information interesting and thought-provoking, if not outright authentic.

In matters of international relations, the extent to which highly qualified persons can be taken in can be seen from the fact that a manuscript fraudulently misrepresented in the United States as the political diary of the former Soviet foreign commissar Maxim Litvinov was adjudged authentic by a number of American experts on the Soviet Union. Former head of the CIA and Undersecretary of State Bedell Smith lent his official prestige to the book by writing a preface to Litvinov's *Diary* when it was published in the United States under the title *Notes of a Journal*. Actually, the manuscript was faked by a former Soviet diplomat who had broken with the Kremlin many years ago and who had fallen upon evil days. This shows how difficult and unsafe is the task of evaluating political information.

This is the reason why Soviet intelligence attributes great importance to knowing the source of the information and to judging it by the degree of the trustworthiness of the informant. And this is why the Soviet intelligence, as a rule, refuses to deal with middlemen who decline to name the source of the material and the person from whom they have procured it. If the documents are very interesting and look genuine, the Russian officer may offer considerably more money than the middleman has asked for, on the condition that he disclose the source and, if necessary, bring the Soviet officer and the informant together. If the middleman is adamant in his refusal, the intelligence officer will play with him for a while, making offers and counteroffers, just for the purpose of trailing him to the person who has access to the secret papers, with the intention of establishing direct contact with him.

The Soviet intelligence does not involve itself in broad research programs which inevitably lead to hypotheses the evaluation of which entails insurmountable difficulties and responsibilities. It works instead with documentary data—procured from the secret councils of foreign governments—in which the intentions and future steps of the governments are spelled out. The evaluation done by the Soviet intelligence concerns itself more with establishing the authenticity of the stolen documents rather than with the significance of the information. The political significance of the information is evaluated principally by the policymaking members of the government and the Party Presidium. To prepare the material for the Politburo there existed in Stalin's times the so-called Little Council of six members (from the NKVD, Intelligence Directorate of the Army and the Commissariat of Foreign Affairs), under chairmanship of Poscriobyshev, chief of Stalin's Secretariat, and Malenkov.